IT'S
COOL
TO BE
CONSCIOUS

Dedicated to anyone who has felt lost and confused,
may some of the ideas in this book help you
on your journey towards light.

IT'S COOL TO BE CONSCIOUS

HARRY O'BRIEN

HAY HOUSE, INC.
Carlsbad, California • New York City
London • Sydney • Johannesburg
Vancouver • Hong Kong • New Delhi

Published and distributed in Australia by: Hay House Australia Pty. Ltd.: www.hayhouse.com.au
Published and distributed in the United States by: Hay House, Inc.: www.hayhouse.com
Published and distributed in the United Kingdom by: Hay House UK, Ltd.: www.hayhouse.co.uk
Published and distributed in South Africa by: Hay House SA (Pty), Ltd.: www.hayhouse.co.za
Distributed in Canada by: Raincoast: www.raincoast.com
Published in India by: Hay House Publishers India: www.hayhouse.co.in

Design by Rhett Nacson
Typeset by Bookhouse, Sydney
Edited by Margie Tubbs
Cover Photography Damian Vincenzi
Stylist Grace Dlabik

ISBN: 9781401938512
Digital ISBN: 9781401933814

16 15 14 13   4 3 2 1
1st Australian edition, November 2013

Printed in Australia by McPherson's Printing Group

CONTENTS

We begin our spiritual understanding in

a mundane place: the ordinary world of

survival—that dimension of tribal or national

consciousness, where the intellect and the ego reign

supreme and tribal attitudes and ideologies are

promoted as the only knowledge one will ever need.

The humdrum plane of the day-to-day existence that

most experience as 'life' is what I call 'tick-tock'.

– Stuart Wilde, *Whispering Winds of Change*

INTRODUCTION

I looked over as I was signing autographs at a personal development event and, out of the corner of my eye, saw a woman. It looked like she was crying. She was holding her phone so that my friend, who had asked me to speak at the conference, could read the message. She looked joyful, although she had tears in her eyes. I quizzed my friend later, asking 'What was that about?' He told me that she'd said that, for as long as she could remember, her teenage son had been telling her that he thought that she was strange—a little bit too 'out there'. When I had looked over at her, she had just sent a photo of herself, with me, to her son. He had messaged straight back 'Mum, maybe there *is* something to what you've been trying to tell me all these years.' And in that moment, I knew that I had to complete this book.

My profile as an AFL player had prompted the boy to go beyond his usual dismissive response to his mother's beliefs. For the first time, he had acknowledged that, if you look at things with fresh eyes, a new path or a new way of thinking may open up.

You've probably picked up this book because you know me as an athlete. I now invite you to journey with me off the field, to explore what I call transcending the surface of life. What I mean by the 'surface of life' is going about your day-to-day life in a trancelike state. We all do it or have been there. I'm going to share with you some of the things I've learnt so far that have helped me go beyond the surface. Let's get started!

GLOSSARY OF HARRY-ISMS

Throughout this book, the terms below will crop up from time to time. A lot of this terminology is in common usage, but I think it's important that you understand where I'm coming from and what my personal spin is. I'd like us to use this language both in the physical and in the 'cool to be Conscious' sense. You'll notice I've used a lot of footy terms. We can all relate to that, no matter what code we follow. So it makes it easy for me to get my point across.

ARENA

The arena is my workplace in the physical, and it's the Conscious place where we can all play for the same team. Unfortunately, not all of us can jump into the arena on weekends—but all of us can occupy the cool Conscious arena by choice.

BOUNDARY LINES

In a game of football, the rules state that we must stay within the boundary lines. When we choose to be Conscious, there are no boundaries except for the ones that we create ourselves.

CONSCIOUS

The Macquarie dictionary defines being Conscious as: *aware of one's own existence, sensations, reasonings, etc.* Rene Descartes said: *I think, therefore I am.* For me, being Conscious is the application of all the senses: taste, sight, touch, sound, and smell. It's about being aware of all that is going on around us; avoiding following the same routine without thinking;

not being controlled by public opinion, stereotypes and judgment; and always being in a position to see beyond the obvious and appreciating that there's always opportunity.

CONSCIOUS REALITY

Reality is what we experience every day: at work, school, university or wherever the day takes us. Conscious Reality is the experience that we have Consciously created.

DHARMA

Dharma occurs when we follow our passion. When something sits with you so easily and purposefully that you wake up each morning smiling, you have found your dharma.

DIABOLICAL

Individuals who intentionally cause pain and suffering to anyone they encounter are the diabolical. Riddled with fear, they are frustrated, petty tyrants who are absolutely fabulous to learn from, because a Conscious person would only do the opposite of what they do.

FOUR QUARTERS

We all know there are four quarters to a game of AFL. There are also four seasons to be experienced every year and I like to live my life by four basic pillars. These pillars make up four important chapters in this book.

GRANDSTAND

One of the main reasons I enjoy playing so much is because of the fans in the grandstand. Whether they're cheering me on or not, the individuals in the grandstand are so important. When I refer to the grandstand in the cool and Conscious context, I speak of individuals who actually have a choice to jump out of their seats and join me in the arena. Of course, when I'm playing footy, there's no opportunity to join me. But when we're on the Conscious path, everyone has an 'access all areas' pass.

INFINITE POSSIBILITIES

The more Conscious you become, the more you'll realise that the world is full of infinite possibilities. Wherever you look, you'll see there's opportunity in everything. Your wishes will be granted and your dreams will come true.

LABELS

Great for items in the kitchen cupboard, but labelling people can stop us from kicking the winning goals we desire. Being Conscious enables you not to make judgements or assumptions. I love the phrase: *there's more to it than meets the eye*. By not putting labels on anyone, you give yourself the opportunity to find out a lot more about an individual or a situation.

MANIFESTING

When we reside in the arena, what's really cool is that we can Consciously create the road to what we desire. Some highly-evolved individuals can do it instantly. But for most of us it's a work in progress, and we are able to manifest a better experience gradually. It's like coming up through the grades and training harder—the more you practise your skills and the more time you spend doing the hard yards, the easier it will be on game day.

MEDITATION

This is one of the most significant tools for getting Conscious and creating calm and clarity in your life and all your experiences. It is the basis of my Pillar 4.

SAGE

I love using this flavoursome herb when I'm cooking. However, it's also the term I give to the many great teachers I've been fortunate enough to meet in person or fortunate enough to meet through their life-changing books. Some great sages who have inspired me are Deepak Chopra, Wayne Dyer and Louise L. Hay. From time to time in this book, I'll be referring to sages. So take it that I'm referring to cool people and not a tasty herb!

WINNING GOALS

The winning goal is that ultimate play. If we're very fortunate, we get a few opportunities to achieve this in our careers. In the cool and Conscious world, the winning goal is achievable in every moment. The ball is always in our hands, there's nothing between us and the goal and we can kick and score whenever we choose.

It's got to be a do-or-die effort. It's got to be a determined effort. You've got to show me all the guts and determination you've got in your body. You've got to inspire me with this last quarter finish. You've been in front all day and you've got to stay there.

EJ (Ted) Whitten, legendary Australian Rules player/coach

THE CONSCIOUS GAME PLAN

The number four has always fascinated me and little did I know how important it would become in my everyday life. As you know, I play a four-quarter game, I love the four different seasons and I have four major pillars by which I live my life. I am all for being Conscious of this experience we call life.

I've always thought that **it's cool to be Conscious**. In my professional life, the team is always looking for the winning goal and I'd like to share with you how to do this in your everyday life. This book is not a step-by-step guide on how to live, because I don't believe there is a right or wrong, better or worse way to go about your business. It's about taking that torpedo punt which travels a long way and lands exactly where you want it.

It's Cool To Be Conscious is based on the understanding that sometimes in life we don't participate; we sit in the grandstand or simply exist outside of the arena. If you exist outside the arena, you're not participating on the playing surface. What I mean by this is that supposedly well-balanced people are going about their day-to-day lives in a purely ritualistic manner—almost like they're in a trance.

Being inside the arena proves to us that we have a choice. We have a choice to see that there's so much more than meets the eye. The vast majority of us believe that the experience we call life is all about choices and decisions. When playing defence, I often have to step back and take an objective look at the game that is unfolding in front of me. I recommend that we do the same in every moment, in order to achieve the desired outcome in our lives that I call Conscious Reality. It's that moment when your game plan, your desires, the unexpected and the magical all occur at exactly the same time, because you've taken a moment to observe before you react.

Problems are created on the field and in life without a game plan. If a team ran out without being Conscious of their opposition, where they're supposed to be and without knowing the rules, it would be a disaster. It's the same in life. If we take on the day in a semi-Conscious manner, we cannot exercise any control over our lives, because we feel we don't have any.

A successful team works together, connects well with one another and each player knows what role they need to perform. The same principle applies if you wish to be successful in anything you choose. On your team are truth, compassion, empathy, confidence, determination and purpose. All these individual aspects of yourself are working towards one goal, to add meaning to your life. That's my definition of being 'Conscious' and I personally think it's the coolest experience one can have.

ENTERING THE ARENA

So how do we gain entry into the arena to find this Conscious way of being? I've found there are many roads you can take. In my life, I've experienced a few particular episodes that have helped me open up.

One occasion stands out in particular. It's the story of

how my mother, my older brother and I came to live in Australia. The decision to move to Australia was due to a promise my father had made to my mother. My father was born in the Democratic Republic of Congo, Africa. At 14, he managed to successfully travel across the border to Angola, where he joined a ballet company. He later left the ballet company, and sought asylum in Rio de Janeiro, eventually migrating to Australia as a refugee. While he was in Rio de Janeiro, he met my mother, who was also a dancer. In this particular part of Rio de Janeiro, an Afro Brazilian dance called Jongo, a mixture of dance and spirituality, was preserved. My father noticed similarities from where he came from and got involved in the dance. My mother was also involved and that's how they met. They had a relationship which didn't work out; but my mother fell pregnant and my father moved to Melbourne, Australia. He worked hard and saved enough money to pay for three tickets for my older brother, my mother and me to come to Australia. So that's how we first got here, through a promise my father had made to bring us to a better life.

The point is that from an early stage in my life, my family could have gone either way. There were two roads, the one in Rio and the unknown road to Australia. My mother had always believed that anything was possible. She knew that by taking a different road, we could experience a better life.

I've been an avid reader all my life. I've picked up great knowledge from reading books by Deepak Chopra, Wayne Dyer and Louise L. Hay amongst others, and from understanding the potent messages of luminaries from all walks of life, such as Martin Luther King and Bob Marley. They have all taught me something and helped me gain a deeper understanding of who I am and why I'm here. These teachings and experiences are the training sessions that have enabled me to gain entry into the arena—the place where we would all like to be. What I'd like to do is illustrate how you can apply the same wisdom to your own life. Throughout this book, I'm going to share with you examples of how I've applied their wisdom to my life and how I've used it to break through boundary lines that, most of the time, we don't even know exist.

Because of my racial/cultural background and my life in the spotlight, some people probably look at my life and consider my experiences as being unique and unorthodox. But each one of us is just as unique and unorthodox. If you understand that, you won't be limited in your aspirations. I believe everyone's life experiences are infinitely unique. I *know* they are unique, because there is nothing that can ever be created the same—similar maybe, but never the same. We can and do put others on a pedestal. And that's okay, as long as you put yourself on the pedestal right next to them. No one needs to be stuck in the grandstand. We all have the same choices as anyone who is in the spotlight.

The experiences that gave me most insight often involved suffering and pain. Turning them from negative experiences into positive outcomes involved my being able to see things from a different perspective—turning the pain and suffering into an understanding of their part in my journey.

I need to train for many hours each week, go through tedious recovery sessions and sometimes play with an injury. By enduring all this, I can see that in the end it makes me a better, stronger player. Again, it's the same in life. We all have challenges and painful experiences and there are so many things we have to do that are unpleasant. It would be really easy to just walk away from them. Once we break through that pain barrier, our inner strength and our self-esteem are elevated, because we've lived and learnt through the experience.

I'd like to share with you one story in particular. There is a favela in Rio de Janeiro called Serrinha, which is rife with violence, drugs and crime. I didn't return to Brazil in my teens, but went back for first time in over ten years in 2006. A lot of people ask what I'd be doing if I were still in Rio De Janeiro, if my mum hadn't come to Australia. I always just say 'I'd be playing soccer.' However, the statistics show it's not like that for every child. The fact is that I'd probably be stuck in poverty. Who knows, I might be involved with crime.

When I go back to Brazil, I'm drawn to *favelas*. These are communities where people face many hardships; but at the same time they seem to be so together and proud of their culture that it gets them through. I look at people who are 14-years-old with AK47 weapons around their neck, whose parents have probably been killed. I also see 12-year-old girls having babies. No matter how lucky I am to have relocated to Australia at a young age, I see myself in these people.

I have a cousin, Hugo, who is two years older than I am. I have a really strong connection with Hugo. He has showed me around the city of Rio and a lot of the time I would think that, if I wasn't in Australia, I'd be there with Hugo. Having said this, during the times I visited him he was unemployed, addicted to cocaine and there didn't seem to be any light at the end of the tunnel. With every visit he appeared a lot worse, still unemployed and addicted to cocaine.

I decided to send Hugo some money to help out the community. However, he took the money and used it to support his drug habit. He was also stealing and selling family possessions. When I found this out I got really angry and confronted him about it. We didn't speak to each other for over a year.

I had a lot of anger inside because of this situation. But as more time passed, I went back there with an open heart. When he saw me he initially thought I was there to get angry with him, but I told him I had left that in the past. I told him he helped me understand the country and my heritage and helped me find my identity. During that particular holiday I spent a lot of time with him, and it was as if we'd never been apart. I asked him if he would like to come to Australia. He laughed and said that it would be great, but I was serious. At that point in time we were sitting at Engenhao soccer stadium, watching our team. At first he thought it was a joke; then he said it would be good to get out of this life, but he'd never even left his community.

I returned to Brazil on a Christmas holiday two months after and I told him it was going to happen. I got him a passport and checked his documents and got him over here to Australia. Hugo has been here for almost two years, no longer takes drugs, studies English and works in a cafe. He now dreams and knows that anything is possible and has even started a Brazilian street clothing label with me! He said he didn't know how he could pay me back for what I've done for him. But I replied that it's not about paying anyone back, it's about paying it forward to someone else.

I felt compelled to help Hugo, because I thought about what my life would be like if I wasn't in Australia, and I saw myself in him. It could have been me, if my mother hadn't taken a chance.

I believe if you can have an impact on someone's life and give someone hope, then they will be a champion of that hope and it will spread like wildfire. You never know, when you plant a seed, the person you help could be the next Nelson Mandela.

One of the key things I now understand is that a lot of individuals choose to sit in the grandstand, happy to watch what's going on in the arena. I call this being semi-Conscious. None of us have all the answers or complete wisdom, but the first step for all of us is to be aware that it's possible to walk out of the grandstand at any time. Whenever we're active in the arena, it's much easier to see the superficial side of life and achieve a deeper knowledge of what really goes on. When you're a Conscious participant in the arena, you're part of the team. You see that you're not separate to the other players, you become one with everyone, you feel connected, and you come to the realisation that anything's possible.

BECOMING CONSCIOUSLY AWARE

From time to time, we sit in the grandstand because of conditioning that has been passed down from generation to generation. Throughout history, people have been seeking ways to develop spiritually and emotionally, and the ones who have taken the leap and found their 'connection with the divine' are the ones who kicked winning goals—what I call the winning goals of life. To kick a goal is to realise that there is splendour and beauty in everything. It's when you see beauty in everyday actions, in people you meet, and you see something positive in every play. I think this is the most important realisation for all of us, and it only comes from understanding that you are wondrous.

But how do you get to this point? In *Manifest Your Desires*, Esther and Jerry Hicks say it doesn't matter what you call your 'Inner Being' or 'Divine Life Source', but it is important that you become Consciously aware of when you are allowing a full connection to it. Their view is that your emotions are constant indicators of whether you're resisting or allowing that connection.

I think some people in the grandstand start to realise this concept, walk towards the arena, feel the soil beneath their feet, but then choose to go back up to the stands. Others express their Conscious connection through music, art, film or sport, by understanding themselves and the true nature of everything. Again, even when you have these amazing experiences where you become Conscious or connected through your art, it's easy to believe your ability to be connected is limited to those occasions when you're expressing your talents. However, it is possible to stay in the arena and keep playing. That's where the suffering is limited or non-existent, and when the ball is in your hands.

I have long admired the self-help author, Louise Hay. She is full of inspiration and one thing she often says is, 'When we expand our thinking and beliefs, our love flows freely. When we contract, we shut ourselves off.'

I totally agree. For me, I find life just works better when I'm Conscious. I would much rather be operating in a Conscious field than only receiving part of the story, which is what happens in the grandstand. Just like in a footy match—you want to play until you hear the final whistle, not just turn up for the first three quarters and go home.

Another way to look at it is to picture yourself actually sitting in the grandstand. All around you is a beautiful arena, and you see other people playing and going about their business. But what if you have the ball and the guernsey and the ability to run onto the field but still stay in the grandstand? You'll just keep seeing the same thing. You'll see the winning kick and be part of the cheering crowd, but this isn't the road to Consciousness, because, in the arena, there's a world of infinite possibilities. As Wayne Dyer says: *You'll see it when you believe it.*

Put one foot on the grass and, as you start getting familiar with the playing surface, you'll see a whole new life—what I call the infinite life. The more you run around the arena, the more you'll see. There has always been a whole other way to experience your life that has always been there. This is when you realise that you can kick a goal whenever you like. The good news is that, once you've kicked one goal, you will be confident enough to kick more and more whenever you choose. Consciousness can be experienced in fleeting moments. But the more time you spend experiencing, those moments will turn into seconds, then minutes, then hours and there will be no full-time siren in your arena.

Each chapter of this book is based on my life and my observations. I would like to adopt the role of a coach, offering personal experience and input from others, so that you can become a confident player in your arena of life. Like any good coach, I have my ideas and those I have acquired from others. I've been fortunate enough to come in contact with the sages, the diabolical, and the everyday person. Everywhere I turn, there is more than what meets the eye. One thing I know for sure is you'll never know the true exhilaration of your own personal arena, if you never leave your grandstand. All you need to do is to make a Conscious move to be in this space more often than you were the day before.

FOREWORD by Dr Wayne W. Dyer:

After spending many years as a family therapist, I've seen how people often become stuck in their habituated modes of thinking, because they fear the criticism that could result if they change.

Living a life of your own involves the unquestioning willingness to endure the slings and arrows that could come your way when you respond to your inner knowing, rather than to the opinions of others.

You don't belong to your immediate family; you are a member of the *human* family. Don't let fear of family dramas, or any dramas, keep you from changing outmoded, necessary and unwanted thought patterns.

I am personally convinced that everyone has a capacity for greatness that transcends anything they've been taught to believe. Allow yourself to look through a new lens by acquiring a set of beliefs that includes your spiritual or God-realised nature.

Ask yourself this question:
If no one told me who I was, who would I be?

PILLAR 1:
SEEK EXPERIENCE TO BECOME MORE CONSCIOUS

Experience tells you what to do;
confidence allows you to do it.

Stan Smith, Grand Slam tennis champion

The **first pillar** is seeking experience. Throughout this chapter, you'll see that your daily experiences, regardless of how eventful they are, give you the opportunity to connect and become more Conscious of what's happening around you.

The key to seeking experience is 'getting out of your comfort zone'. I'm going to give you tips on how to seek experience. I've included my own personal experiences, as well as the incredible experiences of others who have managed to move beyond their comfort zone and witness their world transform.

The following statement has been repeated many times, and it's attributed to Teilhard de Chardin:

We are not human beings having a spiritual experience;
we are spiritual beings having a human experience.

THE IMPORTANCE OF CHOICE

Everything we do in life is full of experiences: some positive, some negative, and worst of all—bland. The one thing that we do have in all of our experiences is choice. We never stop relating to the world. Although you may not think of it as such, waking up after a good night's sleep is an experience. There are the mundane experiences of showering, shaving and going to the bathroom. Although boring, these are nevertheless experiences.

The great thing is that we get to **choose** our experiences. When we make Conscious choices, the experiences are definitely more to our liking. For example, you can look out the window and think it's an awful day, or you can just say it's raining and windy today. The point is, it's your choice as to how you're going to experience the rest of the day, and how you're going to process it in your mind and relay that on to others. It starts with a positive outlook and anticipation for what's ahead. Every sage tells us about the vastness of life, and how we are part of a universal process that can be observed.

Relating this to football, you know your potential as a player, so you realise that if you show up in a positive way on game day, you will have every opportunity to win a match. You realise that it's not only you: you're part of this great big team that's on the field and off the field. There's a greater administration body that is unseen but is constantly working in the same direction as you. There you are, in the middle of the arena. If you take a moment to realise how connected you are to everybody, then in that moment you will savour the experience of not only being an individual, but also being part of the collective Consciousness.

In life, as in the arena, there are infinite ways in which we can express ourselves. I often use the word 'experience'. In my battered old dictionary, one of the definitions of experience is: *knowledge or practical wisdom gained from what one has observed, encountered, or undergone.* I take that to mean that everything I observe; everything that I have encountered; and everything that I've undergone, felt, tasted, heard, and seen is an experience.

Here's what's important: actually taking the time to observe and savour an experience as it happens.

Arthur Ashe, a famous tennis player, once said: *Success is not a destination, it's a journey.*

But I think it should be: *Success is not a destination; it's the <u>experience</u> of the journey.*

There is an infinite number of ways that we can express ourselves, and there is an infinite array of experiences that naturally occur in every moment.

GETTING OUT OF THE COMFORT ZONE

So how do we become Conscious enough to discover that we can make a positive change to our experience? A great way is to be aware of the infinite number of experiences that are available. I'm going to recommend one of my favourite ways to do this: **to get out of your comfort zone**. Our comfort zone is that place where we feel secure and in control. The problem with our comfort zone is it lacks new experiences and opportunities.

Albert Einstein once said: *The only source of knowledge is experience.*

This explains why always seeking an opportunity to have different experiences is crucial to our evolution as human beings. Each and every experience we have, whether positive, negative or bland is, according to Albert Einstein, a 'source of knowledge.' There is a great truth to this, when you think about it. If you continue to choose to have the same experiences time and time again, you will be drinking from the same fountain of knowledge every time.

What I challenge you to do is, at least once a day, try to go beyond what is comfortable. This doesn't have to be a big thing. You might feel comfortable ordering a cup of tea while reading your favourite newspaper at a cafe nearby. Get out of your comfort zone, wander down to a completely new cafe, order an espresso and start reading a lifestyle magazine. This may not sound very challenging, but think of all the different experiences: the experience of location, a different taste sensation and a completely different knowledge. You're out of your comfort zone, where the barista knows your name and what you like; and you have the experience of lining up in a new place and changing the way you experience the day. This can be very empowering. I don't care if you choose not to experience it again—what I want to emphasise is to have the experience. You never know, you may never drink another cup of tea again!

I've never believed the saying 'you can't teach an old dog new tricks.' Cesar Millan, American dog trainer, does it every day of the week, right before your eyes, in his television show called *The Dog Whisperer*. You can be your very own Conscious coach. Any old habits, unproductive patterns and ego-based emotions can be diminished to a point where they're no longer part of your personality, your experience and no longer part of your Conscious game plan.

I enjoy working with anyone who is younger than I am. The young men and women that I meet are fortunate, because they don't have as much conditioning to retract. When you're younger you're in a great space, because you still have the opportunity to create your adult world along the way. Having said this, it doesn't matter how old or young you are, you can always change your universe.

A simple way of seeking a new experience could be to start a conversation with a total stranger with no attachment. For example, you may be on the way to a football game, sitting opposite a total stranger on the train. The one thing you're certain of is that they're supporting the opposition, because of what they're wearing. You could ignore them and cast them the odd dirty look every now and then, or you could seek the new experience. Simply engage them in a conversation: 'How do you think you'll go today?' This immediately gets you out of the grandstand and both into the arena. I know that this is really challenging if they're not wearing the same colours as you, because some fans get aggressive. So try it with individuals that you don't know are supporters of your club. It works the same way.

I know of a case where two strangers started talking, and one found out that the other was in the profession that he desired to enter. By starting up a conversation, he actually got an interview. Another true story is that a friend of mine started talking to someone who happened to work for a recruitment agency. The conversation came round to the fact that he needed a bookkeeper and the other person said, 'I've got half a dozen applicants sitting on file looking for a good company to work for.' The point is, in both cases, no-one would have been in a better position if they hadn't taken the opportunity to experience a conversation with a complete stranger. This is how things start in a small way, just as the Grand Canyon must have started somewhere as a little crack in the ground.

There are situations where the act of seeking a different experience or, going beyond your limitation, actually changes the course of your whole life. Someone I call a sage, Deepak Chopra, was a doctor working in one of the busiest hospitals in the USA. At the time, he was a chain smoker. During a break, he went for a walk and happened to notice a sign taped to a telegraph pole. It caught his attention because it was one of those notices that had been cut up along the bottom, so that a phone number can be easily torn off and taken away. The sign simply said *Quit Smoking*. He removed the phone number, booked in to find out more and it turned out to be a meditation class. He learned to meditate and then he learnt how to teach others to meditate. Deepak Chopra then went on to write a book about the values of meditation, and now he's one of the bestselling authors in the world. My point here is that, by stepping out of his normal comfort zone of having a smoke on the hospital grounds; by going out of his way to read a sign on a telegraph pole; by actually taking the number, making a booking and showing up to a class; a world beyond Deepak Chopra's (or anyone else's) imagination opened up.

I can't impress upon you enough just how important it is to look for what appears to be insignificantly small experiences, then follow them through—like the crack at one end of the Grand Canyon, this could lead to a true wonder of the natural world!

With these thoughts in mind, you're already on your way to becoming even more Conscious. We've all heard the term 'the world is your oyster' (even though you may not be partial to a dozen, with a squeeze of lemon and a sprinkle of salt and pepper). I think that this expression was meant to imply that you just might end up with a pearl!

Travelling is perhaps one of the greatest experiences we have available to us. There was a time where it was difficult; but these days, with all the budget travel options and agencies, it is not out of reach for most of us. It's easy to stay in your comfort zone and travel to the same place over and over again. That's fine if you want to do it, but I recommend that, on every trip, you go somewhere different. Even if it's a side trip, it's still worth the time and energy.

If Bali is your favourite place for a holiday, why not try travel to the other side of the island, or a neighbouring island? I guarantee that you'll feel uneasy at first—it's a new airport, a different hotel and there's nothing familiar. However, no-one can guarantee the experience that may result. It is possible that you'll find a better place to spend your time, more interesting people and a point of difference from what you've previously experienced. The least that will happen is that you'll definitely pat yourself on the back for trying something new. I ensure you that, during my many national and international trips, I try go to ensure I am getting out of my comfort zone.

I'd like to share a story with you about a trip I took to Trinidad in 2009. That year was a very difficult one for me. In early 2009, with only weeks before my first game of the season, I faced a family tragedy. I lost my stepfather, who I considered was my Dad. I took leave for just over one week, before returning to training and playing.

The 2009 season was extremely challenging for me in every way possible, dealing with that great loss to my family. When the season ended, I was well in need of some time to get away. I decided I would go somewhere completely different.

I spent many days spinning my world globe. Every time I did so, I would feel a pull to the Caribbean. I decided to do a little research on the Caribbean and ended up choosing that region for my holiday destination. Firstly I would set off to Trinidad, followed by Tobago and then Barbados. During my research, I discovered just how many islands there were in the Caribbean, each with its own uniqueness. Trinidad seemed like the country where I could completely immerse myself in a totally different culture, where I would be out of my comfort zone. I chose Barbados, because it was only a short journey from Trinidad and has a reputation for being chilled out and very relaxing; two things I was very much in need of at that time.

After two days of travelling from Melbourne Australia, I finally arrived in Port of Spain, Trinidad. As soon as I stepped out onto Trinidadian soil, I was completely out of my comfort zone. Hopping off the plane onto the runway, a mixture of a strong breeze and high humidity made its presence felt—I felt as though I had just entered a fan-forced oven. Then, as the customs officer asked for my passport in her strong Trinidadian accent which left me completely puzzled, I knew I was very far away from what I was used to.

As each day passed in my travels, I felt my awareness expanding. I was able to connect with the people, through universal languages such as food, sport and music. I was rapidly learning about different cultures and found many similarities that I shared with the local people. I was able to celebrate the many differences we had too.

While spending time at the beach in Maracas Bay in Trinidad, I met a Rasta named Dane. He turned out to be a great messenger for my life. At first, I was intrigued by his long dreadlocks and large stature. There he was, with the Caribbean sun shining on his shirtless body, sweeping the outside of a kiosk with a broom. I had initially gone to this kiosk in search of a coconut. Later, I would spend time at this kiosk hearing the valuable wisdom he had to share.

As I waited for my coconut to be opened, I found myself lost in the reggae music being played by the kiosk's radio. As I looked at my surroundings, my eyes locked with Dane's. He looked into my eyes and asked me if I was a fan of reggae. I replied 'Yes' and he gave me a look of satisfaction and said 'That's cool, mon!'

As we got talking, I had a chance to ask him about his beliefs and world views. He spoke to me about the primary value of his life being 'one love': a belief that everyone is equal and connected and so should be treated that way. I learnt about his religion as a Bobo Shanti Rastafari, a religion that I never even knew existed! Not being exposed to this knowledge and experience before, my original perception of Rastas (as just being dreadlocked people who smoked marijuana) began to transform.

After I had spent a couple of days soaking in everything Dane had to tell me, I felt more connected to the world we live in than I had ever felt before. The final thing Dane shared with me is something I carry with me as I write these words. I asked him, 'Why the dreadlocks?' His reply was like music to my ears; the exact words I needed to hear at that particular moment in my life. He told me that he just let his hair run its own natural course and the dreadlocks grew naturally. He said that sometimes in life we get so caught up trying to control everything; we seem to always be in search of material things that will bring us temporary happiness. He said that we don't understand that most of the time we interfere with natural processes and we need to know when to stop trying to play God. He spoke of pain and how we will all experience pain and suffering at times in our lives and that they are natural feelings and will always pass. 'You have to experience darkness to know what true light is,' he said. Dane made such an impact on my life. From that day forward, I decided to let my afro hair grow naturally and the result—dreadlocks!

Today, my dreadlocks serve me as a reminder of the pain of losing my stepfather to suicide and that I have been able to turn tragedy into triumph. But most importantly, they symbolise the messages that I needed to hear at that exact time, from a 'divine stranger' that I met by travelling out of my comfort zone.

I knew I needed some time out, from the demands of my job and from the pain of losing my stepfather. I found it by getting out of my comfort zone and taking the chance to connect with someone I didn't know, from a place where I'd never been. If I hadn't spun my world globe, hopped on a plane, travelled for two days and had the courage to connect with a stranger, I wouldn't have heard the words that meant so much to me at the time I needed them most. When I reflect on those words, 'You have to experience darkness to know what true light is,' I realise that so many of us would benefit from hearing them. It's experiences like this that have driven me to write this book, so I can share the wise knowledge of the messengers that I have encountered so far in my life's journey.

On a smaller scale, you can start by just getting out of your comfort zone the next time you go to your place of work or place of education. Rather than take the same route every time, why not mix it up? Why not take a turn and drive down a road you have never been down, or walk down a path that you always seem to pass by, never knowing exactly where it leads? You can go to a completely different restaurant. Try a cuisine that you have not tasted before or one that you may have tried many years ago. Find a restaurant in a neighbourhood that you don't usually frequent and ask for a menu of dishes that you don't usually eat. This is all about comfort zones, new experiences, new tastes and new friendships. Some of these are available at your favourite corner restaurant; but all of them are available at the restaurant called 'I've Never Been Here Before.'

Getting out of your comfort zone is a leap of faith. Neil Armstrong is famous for saying, 'That's one small step for a man, one giant leap for mankind.' I want you to think of it in the same terms. It's a tiny little step out of the grandstand, but it's a huge leap into the Conscious arena, where you become more and more Conscious of your choices and more aware of what adds meaning to your life.

We are so fortunate to live in an age where acquiring information can be as simple as clicking a button. We live in the age of infinite information, which is made available to most of us on this planet. I have been to Third World countries that have access to the World Wide Web. This tool has made the world smaller—we've all heard this, but it is absolutely true. Someone from Mozambique can now speak to someone in Flagstaff, Arizona. The world has become so much smaller and it's incredible. Not only can we interact; we can also learn about different places. Whether countries or cultures, it all adds to your experiences. Make it your business to do this, and you will see the world open up to you: the world of infinite possibilities.

THINKING WITHOUT LIMITS

I believe that the modern technology of today has thrown the notion of six degrees of separation out the window. I believe the world we live in has few limits and that we are one degree of separation away from anyone who inhabits the planet. Of course, theoretically this is not completely accurate, as there are some things out of our reach. But what you will often find is that we tend to place limits before even trying. For example, if I were to set someone a challenge of getting in contact with the Queen of England, most people would tell me that it is impossible. But why is it impossible? Some will say things like, 'She is too busy to have time for people like me; I'm a nobody,' or 'How on earth could I ever do that?' This is where we break down, placing limits before even trying.

Let's get one thing straight: you are truly divine and amazing! Never forget that fact. You're divine because you have the ability to create things or situations you desire. As human beings, we have the power to think of something; therefore it exists in our minds. We then bring the non-visible into the physical world through creation. That is divinity at its greatest! I will explain the Conscious creation process in the next chapter.

Thinking without limits is something I have always tried to practise. I believe that no one in this world is beyond reach, even the Queen of England herself! Having this belief, and following it up with my actions, has led me to amazing people and places. In 2010, I had the privilege of being invited to make an address at the 63rd Annual United Nations Department of Information Non-Government Organisation Conference, which just so happened to be held in Melbourne. I was invited to speak because of the work I have done in Africa and my advocacy of global health. I was so honoured to have been given such an amazing opportunity. After preparing my speech, I decided that I would love to have someone who has had great experience in global health read my speech and give me some feedback. Straight away Nobel Peace Prize winner Nelson Mandela came to mind. I thought, 'How awesome would it be to have a Nobel Peace Prize winner read my speech?'

Rather than just have this idea exist in my imagination, I decided that I would make it become a reality. I went online and typed 'Nelson Mandela' into Google and immediately found his official website. I then found a contact number on the website and decided that I would buy Skype credit and make a call to that phone number during South African business hours. I rehearsed what I was going to say a couple of times before giving it a try. The phone rang four times, and then was answered by a lady with a strong South African accent: 'Good morning, how can I help you?' I rattled off my rehearsed lines, telling her about how privileged I was to have been asked to speak at the United Nations Conference and that I would love to have Mr. Mandela give me feedback on my speech. She then replied saying, 'I am so sorry but Mr. Mandela no longer works, as he is retired.' I thanked her for her time and hung up.

This didn't deter me and I thought, 'Oh well, at least I tried. Who else can I try?' Seeing as I was in the frame of mind for thinking about Nobel Peace Prize winners, I decided to try another one. I thought straight away of Mr. Mandela's compatriot, Archbishop Desmond Tutu. I followed exactly the same routine, typing his name into Google and finding a contact number from his official website. I then dialled the number and a very polite South African man answered the phone. I introduced myself and used the same rehearsed routine as before. The man paused for a moment and then gave me another number to contact. He told me it was the number for Dan, Archbishop Tutu's personal assistant. I thanked him and ended the call. I called the number I was given, and a man who introduced himself as Dan Vaughn answered. After explaining to him the reason for my call, he gave me his email address and asked me to send him my speech and he assured that he would see what he could do. The next day I received an email from Dan, telling me that he had given Archbishop Tutu my speech, and that I could expect a reply in the coming days. I was absolutely amazed and felt a huge sense of connection to the world and everyone in it. I thought to myself, 'A Nobel Peace Prize winner has my speech in his hands and will read it. Wow!' After two days, I received another email from Dan. This time it contained a personal message from Archbishop Tutu himself:

Dear Heritier
I have had a response from Archbishop Tutu. This is what he says:

> *'Dear Heritier, thank you for your contribution towards the alleviation of the suffering of humankind. I commend you for your passion on behalf of others and wish you well in the presentation of your address at the Conference, as well as your future endeavours to this end. God Bless You, Archbishop Emeritus D M Tutu.'*

I hope this suits your purposes. Please let me know.
Best, Dan

I was so amazed and grateful for this response. I had proved to myself that thinking without limits can get you anywhere. So I encourage everyone to try new things. You'll be able to share what you've learnt with your friends, work colleagues, family and even strangers, in the same way that I have shared my story about Archbishop Tutu. It may even be the very thing that determines whether or not you get that dream job. If you have questions about something you're going through; perhaps you've lost someone close to you; perhaps you're feeling run down and overworked; or maybe you're just looking for a life change. The point is that, if you have questions, chances are you'll find answers. You will find answers to everything by getting Conscious. When you seek, you shall find.

CONSCIOUS TIPS TO REMEMBER

- Everything you do in life is full of experiences. It's up to you to Consciously choose your experiences, or at least choose your feelings in relation to an experience.
- Consciously choose to start the morning with positivity, and the rest of the day will follow suit.
- Be Consciously aware of everything you observe, encounter, undergo, feel, taste, hear and see. These are all experiences.
- Feel confident, knowing that the experiences you can have are infinite.
- Open yourself up to all opportunities and experiences, by taking yourself out of your comfort zone. Start off with something small, like choosing to experience a new cafe.
- Take a chance and strike up a conversation with someone you don't know. You never know where the exchange of energy and information may lead you.
- It's never too late to change your universe. Be your own Conscious coach and eliminate unproductive patterns and old habits that no longer serve you and your new Conscious game plan.
- Travel to a new destination, and watch as new experiences start rolling in.
- Make it your business to try new things and share your experiences with your family and friends.
- Don't fear the unknown, embrace it!
- Seek and you shall find.

FOREWORD by Louise L. Hay:

The thoughts we choose to think are the tools we use to paint the canvas of our lives.

I learnt a long time ago that the wisdom and understanding of Spirit resides in me, and I am divinely guided at all times. Just as the stars and planets are in their perfect orbit, I am also in my divine right order.

I may not understand everything with my limited human mind; however I know I am in the right place at the right time, doing the right thing.

Who are you? What did you come here to learn? What did you come here to teach? We all have a unique purpose. We are more than our personalities, and we are far more than our bodies. We are all spirit, light, energy and love, and we all have the power to live our lives with purpose and meaning.

As we learn to love ourselves and trust our Higher Power, we become co-creators with the Infinite Spirit of a loving world. The wisdom and intelligence of the Universe is yours to use. Trust the power within you to be there for you.

PILLAR 2:
UNDERSTAND THE CONSCIOUS CREATION PROCESS

> *'It's hard to beat a person*
> *who never gives up.'*
>
> Babe Ruth, legendary US baseball player

The **second pillar** is the Conscious Creation Process. This chapter will give you the tools to understand what it means to Consciously create and show how you can apply this to your life. Firstly, I'm going to stress the importance of finding your passion. I'm also going to encourage you to rethink the way you feel about intelligence, which may just change the way you feel about going after your passion. Finally, I'm going to introduce you to my 3-step process to Consciously creating.

FIND YOUR PASSION

Imagine waking up every morning with a smile on your face, knowing you're helping to make the world a better place. This happens when you are following your dharma or, as I like to call it, following your passion.

The Dalai Lama says that the main aim of the practice of dharma is to train the mind. He says dharma, in the true Buddhist sense, is about transforming our hearts and dissolving any bad feelings we have towards others. Like when someone is angry towards you—you have a choice whether to react to it with anger, or just let it go, and show them love instead.

I agree with the Dalai Lama's belief that it's important to offer love and compassion to others, no matter how they treat you. You never know what a person may be going through or dealing with at that point in their lives. In an ideal world, I'm sure we'd all prefer it if people were kind to us all the time.

One of my favorite personal 'love' stories, which occurred in early 2009, really helped me realise just how important acting with love can be. I had received a call from my mother, who at the time lived in Perth with the rest of my family. When I answered her call, I realised immediately from the distressed tone of her voice that something was wrong. She began to share with me her recent discovery of my stepfather's financial transgressions, which had left my family completely vulnerable.

My immediate emotional reactions were of anger, fear and sorrow. I was angry because I felt that my stepfather had betrayed the trust of all of us, by making poor decisions that would affect us all. That anger developed into a great sense of fear; fear of the unknown ramifications his actions would have on our family and the shame it could bring to our family, possibly tarnishing all of our lives.

Then my imagination kicked in in a way that seemed out of my control. My mind began to form a myriad of 'probable realities' and seemed to engage itself in a dialogue that was beyond my Conscious influence. 'Will we lose everything? Will I have to sacrifice my entire life savings? But I've worked my f---ing ass off here in Melbourne, basically starting from nothing to be earning good money! That's f---ing bulls---t. I'm not giving up anything for his mistakes. But what about my little brother and sister? They shouldn't have to suffer, should they...?'

I had become a prisoner of my own subjective mind. This was not 'love'. I decided to act on those emotions with a phone call to my stepfather.

Me: 'Dad, what the hell is going on? What have you done?' ... Silence ...

'Well, be a man and F---ING ANSWER ME!'

He replied by saying, 'I can't and won't tell you the extent of it all, but I've f---ed up.'

Me: 'How the f--- could you do this to us all?'

Dad: 'Just listen to me. Don't get involved. Keep what you have worked hard for in Melbourne.'

I swiftly responded with, 'You're the last f---ing person I will ever take advice from.'

I then hung up. Moments later I sat and thought about the phone call I had made to my stepfather and what I had achieved from it— and the answer was absolutely nothing. Nothing positive came from that phone call.

My feelings of anger, fear and sorrow were not eradicated by that phone call. Rather, I had transmitted those feelings on to my stepfather, which would have no doubt exacerbated the pain he was already feeling. The more that I reflected on the situation, the more I remembered the infinite power of love and how it had worked wonders, not only in my life, but in the lives of many great people throughout history who have moved mountains.

I remembered the role that the unconditional love of my mother and stepfather had played in my life. A newborn baby cannot survive without the unconditional love it receives from those who care for it. And the unconditional love my mother gave me that was essential to giving me life as an infant has never ceased. My stepfather, on the other hand, was not my biological father. He was a white Australian. He looked nothing like me; in fact, he was the polar opposite. He owed nothing to me. He married my mother, not me. He didn't have to try to be anything more. But he did.

One example which illustrates how he thought was when we were at the airport together as a family, waiting for him to board a flight. A rude man asked him, so that all of us could hear, 'So you're a father to those and a stepfather to the black one?' Dad looked this man straight in the eyes and said, with enormous conviction, 'I'm a father to them all. They are *my* kids'. I quickly remembered that love is the foundation of human life. I had seen it work miracles throughout my whole life, setting free all those who chose its power.

So I quickly picked up my phone with a new sense of purpose and pushed the redial button. My stepfather answered the phone, still evidently affected by the last call. That is when I told him straight away that I loved him. I could hear him sobbing while I struggled to articulate in the midst of the extreme emotion: 'Dad, despite the mistakes you have made, I will always love you with all my heart. I am so sorry, I love you so much.' He replied with, 'I love you too. I am so sorry for everything. I love you.' I told him not to be sorry and ended the phone call by once again telling him that I loved him.

That was the last time I ever spoke to my stepfather. The next day he ended his life. The police found his body a week later.

Unconditional love has allowed me to share a story of great pride and fulfilment, rather than a story of deep regret and sorrow. I am eternally grateful I chose love.

As well as showing love to all beings, I also refer to dharma as our passion. I believe that if you are able to find the goals that you're meant to kick (your dharma), then you will be able to start removing some of life's drama and everything will become easier. When you know you are fulfilling your purpose or following your passion, life offers you natural opportunities for creativity and you feel more comfortable sharing your uniqueness. Once you are on your path, you will notice the infinite possibilities that come with that knowledge.

Finding your passion can give you a new sense of liberation. You'll escape the daily grind and you'll find more encounters along your journey, discovering opportunities and possibilities along the way.

For me, finding my passion was critical. If it wasn't for sport and music, I'd be lost. When I'm playing on the field or listening to music, I feel completely Conscious and in the moment, ready to take on the world. I just know these two things are part of who I am. If I wasn't playing footy, I'd either be helping others to find their passion, or working in the music industry.

Finding your passion allows you to explore different ways of expressing yourself. If your passion is for making music, then there are many ways in which you can express yourself besides singing or playing a musical instrument. You may get a job working behind the scenes on the sound desk, or in a studio putting the final production together.

I read an interesting article on Anders Ericsson's 10,000-Hour Rule. Through his research, Ericsson found that high achievers in areas such as music and sport weren't necessarily born with an exceptional gift, but have been extremely dedicated and have put an enormous amount of practice into their art. The point is, opportunities to excel are open to anyone willing to put in the time and practice. This can take years—hence the 10,000 hours, which is spread up to and over 10 years.

Ericsson's theory made me think of possible reasons why some people think they're unable to achieve their dreams or to find and follow their passions. Many of us think that the talented people we hear about, read about and see in the media were born with amazing gifts that we'll never possess. I'm not saying that certain people aren't born with a gift for music or sport or whatever it is that they're known for. I'm simply saying that we, too, have the opportunity to follow our dreams if we want to; to make the decision that we want to excel in something we love; and to put in the hard work to reach our goal. We might have to go above and beyond in practice and, of course, be prepared to fail initially. But that's all part of the experience which will ultimately be extremely exciting. Always remember, when you're Consciously thinking of what it is that you love doing, you discover that there's a number of ways you can express yourself. This is where the fun begins.

I've heard a lot of people say they don't know what they're passionate about; they don't know what it is that makes their heart beat. If you know your passion, you're already halfway there. But for those of you who don't know what your passion is, start by thinking what it is that makes you tick. Write it down on a piece of paper; you might be surprised what you come up with. I know it's not always an easy task, so I'd like to share with you how I found mine.

But before I talk about my passion specifically, I'd like to share with you a little story about when I first came to Australia. When I first arrived in Australia in 1989 with my mother and older brother, we lived in Fitzroy in housing commission accommodation. At that time, my mother worked as a welder in a factory to support us. Despite the difficulties she faced, I'm grateful for what she always continued to tell me: *No matter what I do, if my heart's in it and I work hard, I can achieve anything.* She repeated this to me almost daily! The repetition at the time was often a nuisance; but when I reflect on those days, the message I was taking in from my mum had actually formed my belief: **the belief that anything is possible.** This message helped to form the basis of what I was capable of doing.

From the age of 15, I knew that I wanted to play professional Australian Football (AFL). Where I lived at the time, all the kids in my neighbourhood and school had the dream of playing football professionally. Being from Brazil, people often asked me why I didn't play soccer. When I was younger, soccer wasn't big and AFL was popular with the kids at school. Also, my stepfather was a fan and introduced a passion for AFL into my family. It wasn't until I grew older that it became more serious, and I made it *my* dream.

While AFL was my dream from the age of 15, I also had another dream: to help those in need. Football would be the platform I needed to be able to help people and to shed light on the misfortunes that so many people in the world experience. My mother always used to remind me, when I was younger, that there's always people who need help. Her message was that the world is full of children who barely have enough food to survive, who are without education or even shelter. This was ingrained into my subconscious, ultimately forming my passion for wanting to help those in need.

Finding my passion was really a combination of things. I can definitely say it stemmed from confidence, and knowing I could do whatever I wanted to do, thanks to my mother's message. Athletic ability also helped me with my football career, and I believe the combination of the two has got me to where I am today. I was fortunate that football worked out for me, but that wasn't always the case.

We have a process called the National Draft. When you're turning 18, you sign a contract that stipulates that you allow any team in the country to pick you. It is almost like a lottery system. Under the National Draft, the 16 teams (at that time) had 90 picks all up, and they chose the talent. As you can imagine, tens of thousands of young men were all hoping to be picked.

2004 was the year of the draft for me. While I'd played representative football in Western Australia, I didn't know if I would be chosen. It really was touch and go; what they were going to see would be very raw. Unlike other kids who knew they'd be selected, I didn't have peace of mind that I'd be picked. On 20th November 2004, I sat around the phone with my family and it was my moment. Deep down I knew that I would become a professional footballer, because I wanted to use that to help people. I sat through the draft right up until 'pick 90.' No-one called my name and I was shattered. My dream disintegrated before my eyes. I became instantly depressed, as well as a bit embarrassed, with all my family there and my friends asking how I went. I felt really rejected. I locked myself away until the next day. But as the sun rose in the morning, as it always does, I had a new sense of passion, belief and hope, because I was programmed to believe that anything was possible. Just because my name wasn't read out, it didn't mean that I couldn't find another avenue. Just because that door was locked, it didn't mean that I wouldn't find a way through. There's always a way, if you keep persisting.

Two days after the National Draft, I took action by going online to the Collingwood Football Club website. I found a hotline and called them from Perth, asking if I could speak to the recruiting manager. The receptionist on the other end was slightly taken aback; perhaps she hadn't had that many direct requests of this kind. Nevertheless, she told me to hold the line. I held on while she connected me, although it went straight to a message bank. I left the message, 'My name is Harry O'Brien, please call me.' Derek called back within half an hour and I said to him, 'Hi Derek, I'm Harry. You may or may not have seen me play. I missed out on the draft and it's always been my dream to play professional AFL.' I told him I was wondering if I could train with the club, if I paid my own way. Derek didn't say 'no', but said that he couldn't promise me anything either. He said that he would speak to those above him.

I remember the moment Derek called me back: 2hours, 13 minutes and 32 seconds later! He said it was no problem for me to train for two weeks. Not even being on the 2004 Rookie Draft, I packed my bags, bought a ticket with the money I'd saved doing work with a nearby indigenous community, rushed to the airport and set off for Melbourne.

I had organised to sleep on a mattress on the floor of a family friend's place and I remember that mattress being very thin. But where I slept didn't matter, as I had my foot in the door of the biggest football club in Australia. My dream of AFL, as well as my dream of helping others, is what drove me to find a way in and there I was. I later moved to another family friend's place, where it took three trams to get to the club. It was a whole new adventure for me. Stepping out of my comfort zone, I saw players I'd watched on TV, including Nathan Buckley, captain of Collingwood and also one of the best players of that time, and I was in awe. While initially I was really nervous, I thought to myself: 'If this is the only opportunity I get to be a professional footballer, I'm going to make the absolute most of it.' I knew I'd done everything possible to ensure my dream stayed alive, and I wasn't even a rookie at that time.

Collingwood coach, Mick Malthouse, said to me, 'Look, we don't expect you to be at the level of these guys in terms of fitness, and don't think we're going to be judging you really harshly if you can't keep up.' After hearing this, I was even more determined to shatter his expectations. I trained really hard, and showed I wasn't just at their level but had the determination to achieve a fitness level that exceeded the lot of them.

RETHINK INTELLIGENCE

There is a link between finding your passion and seeking new experiences, as mentioned earlier. When you seek experience, you will learn which experiences are valuable to you and which of them give you little motivation. We live in a society where the paradigm for education is specifically based around memory, rather than asking questions. If we asked more questions about ourselves, and we were put in situations that encouraged self-reflection, we would gain a better understanding of it. Self-reflection is a wonderful way to help find your passion, not to mention an excellent way to become more Conscious.

Self-reflection is a very important part of my life and has been for a long time. I have been very fortunate, because football has taught me many amazing lessons that I can emulate in my day-to-day life.

In any sport, it is crucial to prepare and evaluate your performance, in order to seek improvement. Any professional athlete's performance is heavily scrutinised by many entities, such as coaches, teammates, media and fans. It is extremely important to act like a filter in the way you take in or discard the thoughts and opinions of others, as they can distort your perception of reality.

Ultimately, you are the creator of your own destiny. So it is extremely important that, beyond all of the external 'noise', you turn your thoughts inwards and reflect on exactly how you feel at a particular point in time. Self-reflection is the key to mastering your own life. Regardless of who you are or what you do, whether you are a professional athlete, a musician or a builder, there will always be people who will want to give you 'advice' on how you should live your life. Now I am not suggesting that you disregard the advice you are currently receiving or will receive in the future. However, I am saying that you must recognise and appreciate the most important person in your life – and that person is **you**.

If you want to control your life and create what you desire, then don't forget to ask yourself from time to time exactly how you feel about your current state of affairs. If you are feeling terrible, rather than just acknowledge the fact that you are down, why not do something about it? You will find that, most of the time, true change starts with you and only you. Ask yourself, 'Why am I feeling this way? What is it in my life that is making me feel awful? What can I do to change things? How can I improve the situation?' These are just some basic questions that people tend to neglect, because they are too busy listening to what others have to say about their life. When things are going well, ask yourself: 'Why they are going so great? What actions or processes are working for me right now?

We have all heard the saying: *Stop and smell the roses.* This has been around for a long time to remind people of a great truth: to appreciate the current state of things while you are in them. I say, 'Stop and smell the roses; but, more importantly, remember how they got there.' Self-reflect, evaluate and access how you got to where you are right now, good or bad.

There is a great saying that always sits in my mind: 'Nothing fails more than success.' This means that, when people achieve a certain level of performance or state of being, they get caught up in the whirlwind of it all and forget about how they got there in the first place. So, soon enough, they see themselves sliding back to where they started or sometimes even worse. I see this happen all the time, whether it is in sport, business or any other area of life.

This is how great empires have fallen, great sporting upsets have occurred, and slides into depression have occurred. Empires and sporting teams throughout history have fallen due to complacency, thinking that they have reached a point where they no longer have to follow the process that got them there in the first place. Opposition teams (or enemies) are always employing self-reflection, to better understand how they can reach the top of the mountain and knock their opponents off. On an individual level, people can slip into a state of depression, if they don't keep a good enough gauge on themselves and their wellbeing.

I was one of these people. I'd like to share with you some thoughts from a time when I had begun to feel the benefits of a regular practice of meditation and self-reflection, which helped me avoid heading towards a state of depression.

In March 2009, three weeks prior to the first game of the AFL season, my stepfather Ralph hung himself. I was on the other side of the country (you'll recall that my family lived in Perth at that time). Being so far away, I had the feeling that something significant was about to happen, after a series of telephone calls from my family. Two weeks after these calls, my stepfather committed suicide.

Ralph left behind a huge mess, emotionally and financially. This 'mess' affected my entire family in a myriad of negative ways. I felt it was my duty to become the 'rock' of the family, the one who would lead the way through example and be a support in every way needed.

Within a week of my stepfather's funeral, I was back in Melbourne preparing to play in our first match of the season. My football club was very understanding and gave me a lot of freedom to do my own thing, to ensure I could cope with the difficult situation I found myself in.

I remember feeling okay. I was actually surprised that I was able to keep it together and function somewhat normally.

The initial phases of the grieving period were extremely difficult and not a day passed when I did not think about everything that had happened. Football was the great facet of my life which allowed me to feel stable. Although at times it was hard keep my mind on the job, I was able to realise the importance it had in my life. By trying to be fully engaged and present when I was at 'work', I was able to give my mind a focus other than the problems I was currently enduring. The discipline required to do my job as best as I could was something that I used as a coping mechanism. Through channelling my energy into another outlet (football) and shifting my mental focus, I discovered how important and effective it is to have control over your own mind.

I began to immerse myself into the journey of under-standing how and why people can lose control of their own minds. The human mind is the most powerful tool we possess; however if not used correctly, it becomes the greatest burden on our lives. Having experienced the tragedy of my stepfather taking his own life, then being faced with the ripple effect of challenges that came my way as a result, I identified that my mind was vulnerable. And, if I did not intervene consciously, it would be my downfall.

I would often wake up with negative thoughts about my life. I would question whether I was up to the challenges and responsibilities of helping my family rise from the ashes. I decided that, in order to counteract the negative thoughts and doubts, I had to take in as many positive things as I could. This would be done through watching inspirational movies, listening to meaningful music, and reading books about how to take control of your life, which is what I ultimately wanted to do. Each empowering book I read made mention of the importance of having a still mind. One book mentioned that the mind is like a lake: it can either be still or wavy and agitated. When the mind is still we can see things more clearly, just as when a lake is calm and still. When the mind is agitated and wavy our reality becomes distorted, and we can often lose full sight of reality.

The more still our minds become, the less suffering we will experience. This is because we have more control over how things affect our nature. I was on a path to discovering how to have a 'still mind', because I wanted to avoid suffering as much as possible.

I came across one particular book by Dr Wayne Dyer that succinctly explained how to achieve stillness of the mind through the use of regular meditation. I have always believed in being proactive, rather than reactive, to situations. Being proactive ensures you are able to prevent something from breaking, instead of waiting for it to be broken before acting. That is why I decided to give regular meditation a try, in the hope that it would prevent me from a downward spiral that could likely result from trying to deal with the death of my stepfather and the challenges that came with it.

I remember at the start that it was extremely difficult. My mind would race with thoughts and I would become extremely agitated and not able to be still for more than ten minutes, let alone the twenty that were recommended.

I meditated inconsistently, meditating for consecutive days then being totally unmotivated to do so on other days. My mind was so unstable that I could not sit still and be at peace without something to keep my mind occupied. This pattern continued for a few months. However, I continued to coincidentally come across information about the importance of a still mind and how the use of meditation as a tool goes hand in hand with it. I became determined to achieve more stillness of mind and learnt various techniques of meditation. The technique that seemed to be the easiest was called Transcendental Meditation. I learnt from a qualified teacher of the practice who was able to guide me through the process. It was extremely easy to pick up and, before I knew it, I was seeing the immediate benefits of being in more control of my mind. I was finally able to understand what 'stillness' of the mind was.

The immediate effects I found were more calmness, increased concentration, increased energy and decreased stress. I was able to notice the benefits so clearly because the tragedy I was grieving over, and the new stresses I was enduring, became easier to cope with. Before, I would spend most of my day thinking about why my stepfather had taken his life and what the ramifications were for me and my family. Being in control did not mean that these worries and stresses completely dissolved, but I was able to have a clear mind and stay more focused on what I was currently doing at the time—mostly my career as a footballer. I have no doubt that, if I had not learnt how to gain control and be proactive with my mental state, I would not have been able to continue to perform at an elite level.

After a couple of months of regular meditation, I began to achieve almost complete stillness of the mind. Every facet of my life felt amazing and, despite the great adversity I was feeling, I felt like a well-oiled machine. I would often think about my stepfather and see the negative impact he had left behind on me and my family. But I was finding I was able to transcend the thoughts quite easily and also begin to find new blessings that would arise from the adversity. I began to speak about my experiences publicly, in the hope of inspiring those who could relate to my story. Despite the suffering I was feeling, I was able to transform the pain into the utter joy that I felt from helping others. This was the hidden blessing.

I had been hit with a lot of adversity in a relatively short period of time, firstly with the suicide of my stepfather, then a plethora of issues that arose after. The clear mind that I was able to achieve through my regular practice of meditation allowed me to function normally, with a mental state resilient enough to overcome the negative effects of major turmoil. I felt almost invincible and began to understand how powerful the human mind really is.

I believe that we all intrinsically understand that self-reflection is vital. That is why the concept of a New Year's resolution is universally recognised. New Year's Eve is an important and sacred time for me. It is a time when I reflect on the year that has passed and, more importantly, take time to begin to create the year that I would like ahead of me. Everything starts off in my mind in thought form. The next step for me is to make sure I concentrate all the thoughts that are swirling around my head by writing down the most prominent ones – the ones that I feel the most emotional connection to. For example, on New Year's Eve 2009 I made note of a clear ambition I had: to become the best player in my position in the country. I wrote that thought down because I felt so strongly about it. It was just a thought but, by concentrating harder on that thought, specific ideas began to appear in my mind about that thought. I began to self-discover what I needed to do in order to achieve that ambition. I was able to see and create the path to becoming the best player in my position. This included the way in which I conducted my life: everything from diet to sleep to the intensity at which I trained. From one simple thought or ambition, I was able to create many other ideas that were related to that specific thought all on my own.

Once I had completed that process, I was able to understand what it was that was making my heart beat at the time. And that was my ambition to be the best. Secondly, I was able to create the initial 'blueprint' for how I would get to that point.

Architects, musicians and authors will all tell you that their initial thought or ambition of what they intended to create, and the blueprint of getting there, does not always end up the way they initially thought. Amazing songwriters and artists, such as Bono of U2, Chris Martin of Coldplay or Jay-Z, have created amazing songs that have gained universal popularity, through reflection of their own reality and experiences. During the process of creation, when you self-reflect you will discover things along the way by accident and learn what is 'good' and 'bad' for you. A director of a film may do hundreds of takes just to get one scene of a movie right. Each time he is self-reflecting on the image that he ideally wanted to create, until he finally achieves it. Be the director of your own life; keep trying to discover the process that works best for you. Ask yourself, why, how, who and what.

This journey is something that you have to start on your own. Along the way, you will find people and things that help you or hold you back. That is why they say that 'beauty exists not in the destination, but in the journey'. And that is because of the amazing process of discovery – self-discovery – and it all begins with **self-reflection**.

After a good session of self-reflection, I urge you to try and disregard your current notion of intelligence. Why do I say this? Well, if you gathered a group of people who went to school together and you asked them who are the most intelligent, the majority of them would point to the same handful of people. If we then asked them why they chose those people, they'd probably say 'because they were A Grade students in maths or science.'

But why is it common to only acclaim a certain form of intelligence, when there are so many ways people can express their talents? What about the students who excel in physical activities or music? Why isn't the violinist in the orchestra, who hits every note perfectly, perceived as being as intelligent as the student who tops physics? These are questions worth considering.

Louise L. Hay talks a lot about reprogramming old tapes, and this is the same thing I'm talking about here. In her book *The Power is Within You*, she mentions a woman she met who wanted to be an actress. However, instead of acting, she had gone to law school because that's what her parents wanted her to do. She dropped out after a month, because it didn't feel right. If we consider intelligence to be law degrees or physics inventions, then we're missing the point. If my parents hadn't encouraged me to follow my passion, who knows where I'd be?

Many people in society are unhappy with their lives because they are following a path that is not for them. From time to time, we all must do things that we don't want to do in our employment. For example, I know many teachers who feel as though they were born to teach and love teaching, however they dread having to grade exam papers. Elite athletes are always pushed by their coaches to train hard, in order to get maximum results. Quite often, this is not a comfortable experience for the athlete and they may tell you that they 'hate' a particular exercise because of the pain it puts them through.

There will always be things that we enjoy more than others and sometimes there will be things that you 'hate' about your job. However, don't fall into the trap of not liking everything you do, as this will just lead to stress and unhappiness.

I know many people who feel uninspired and resentful towards their jobs, and these negative feelings ultimately end up affecting their quality of life. I have one particular friend who is a talented painter and passionate about art; however that friend studied business/marketing at university, because many people (including his parents) told him that there was no money in art and that he should do a course that is 'versatile' and 'respectable'. He often fantasises about what life would have been like if he had decided to further develop his artistic talents, instead of succumbing to the pressure of those around him.

My artistic friend literally starts his days by saying 'F---!' as he turns his alarm off, because he thinks about the day he has to endure. He listens to morning radio as he sits in traffic in his car while sipping on a strong coffee to give him a caffeine boost for what is to come. He describes his job as being the major contributing factor in an 'uninspiring existence'. After a day on the 'grind' he gets home and feels completely and utterly drained and thanks God that the experience is over. Nowadays, he rarely creates artwork. This is a real shame because he describes it as being something that he really enjoys and which makes him feel inspired. I guess he has fallen into a rut and become another product of the rat race.

Quite often I ask him why he continues to persist with the job he is in and he always tells me that it is because it gives him security. 'It pays the bills' is his usual reply. He also mentions that he could possibly get promoted and climb his way up the ladder and begin to earn double the amount he is earning.

Often, we are caught up in the world that other people consider to be 'intelligent.' We need to rethink our current view, so we can regain a sense of self-worth. Once you rethink what intelligence means to you, your personal skill set (which may have been considered by you as 'not good enough' or 'not intelligent') may now be given the tick of approval.

A great way to rethink intelligence is to reflect on the theory of intelligence proposed by Harvard academic, Dr.

Howard Gardner. In 1983, Dr. Howard Gardner coined the term 'multiple intelligences.' He concluded that the current paradigm of intelligence, and the way we esteem people with intelligence, is too limiting. His theory is based on the fact there are so many categories of intelligence that it's impossible to define intelligence by academic proficiency alone. In our current society, it's generally people with a logical mathematical talent or a linguistic talent who are considered the most intelligent.

In actual fact, there are many forms of intelligence. Dr. Gardner was one of the first to openly acknowledge that there are eight different types. I believe it's still limiting to be categorising them at all, but our rational minds find it useful to create categories of intelligence, as it helps us to understand the concept.

In any case, saying there are eight different kinds of intelligence, as Dr. Howard Gardner suggests, is a far better way of looking at things than our current idea of one: academic intelligence. If you're someone with no talent for mathematics, but can play the guitar like Jimi Hendrix, then consider that as your 'intelligence'. Being artistic is as much of a talent as being good at algebra, and it's a way to help you find real passion in your life. Passion is a powerful motivator and can really help you find your true path.

At the moment, we don't esteem those with musical or sporting talents enough. But understanding that there are multiple intelligences is a great way of understanding yourself. Which categories do you fit into? The eight categories that Dr. Gardner talks about are:

LINGUISTIC INTELLIGENCE

the use of language to express yourself effectively

BODILY-KINAESTHETIC INTELLIGENCE

the potential to use your body to solve problems and coordinate the body during movement

LOGICAL-MATHEMATICAL INTELLIGENCE

the ability to analyse problems logically and carry out mathematical operations

INTERPERSONAL INTELLIGENCE

the capacity to understand the intentions, motivations and desires of others

INTRAPERSONAL INTELLIGENCE

the capacity to understand oneself and appreciate our own feelings and fears

MUSICAL INTELLIGENCE

skill in performing, composing and appreciating musical patterns

SPATIAL INTELLIGENCE

the potential to recognise and use the patterns of wide or confined space

NATURALIST INTELLIGENCE

the ability to connect with nature and make use of natural resources

Every form of intelligence has its own merits but, even though this is a starting point, it's not the full story. The capability of human beings is immeasurable. The moment you begin to limit or put yourself in a single category (like being good at mathematics or sport), you begin to rule out possibilities for other things. Understanding that there are multiple intelligences is a start, but it's better not to limit yourself to one. By not limiting yourself, you will start to see the possibilities that being Conscious can bring.

Starting to change your perception on intelligence might just help you on your way to discovering your passion. Previous hang-ups, which you may have held on to due to what other people thought, may be eliminated. Then what you're truly passionate about can shine through. This is when the Conscious creation process begins.

TAKE CONTROL OF YOUR LIFE

How good would it be if you could be responsible for everything in your life and everything that happens in your life? It would be amazing if you could get control of that, wouldn't it? Of course there are things that are left to you. A lot of people think that life is not up to them, that life just happens around them. Well, the truth is: you are life, and you create life. So, in fact, we actually do have control of the creation process. We are creative creatures. We can create anything that we set our minds to, absolutely anything. We have not seen anywhere near the ceiling of what human beings can create. If you had said, before the Wright Brothers invented flight, that humans would be able to fly, people would've laughed at you. The same can happen for any concept that exists, even teleportation, which many people scoff at. But who's to say that it's not possible? I believe anything is possible.

Now, I don't just believe it—I know it—because of my passion for football. I followed my dream and it became a reality, because I worked hard and thoroughly believed it would. During my first two weeks of training with Collingwood Football Club, one of the players, Paul Licuria, known as being one of the nicest guys in football, took a liking to me straight away. The way he got to play AFL was through hard work, not necessarily talent, and he may have seen that in me. Paul taught me a lot about how you should treat people. He took the time to sow a few seeds that he probably didn't benefit from, but that benefited me greatly. I was so grateful to meet someone else who believed in helping others, another person who understood how important the Conscious creation process is.

Now the reason why understanding the Conscious creation process is crucial is because, when you understand how it works and understand the way things manifest into reality, you gain an appreciation of your own true divinity. You'll then realise that you have control over everything that comes your way. As I mentioned earlier, we have a choice about creating everything that comes our way. Now some of us are exceptional at creating; others are not so good in certain areas. Some people are good at creating things in certain areas of their lives, perhaps wealth or financial success, but may be poor in creating other areas, such as happiness with their family. None of this is an issue, because this can be changed. The reason why it's so important to understand the creative process is so you can use it in your life.

I'd like to share with you an example of a period during which I relinquished control of my life, and had to make a Conscious effort to get things back on track.

A high level of discipline is required to play sport at an elite level and, to perform with success, a healthy lifestyle must be followed. You must forgo many pleasures that non-athletes enjoy, such as a highly active social life. It is normal when the season is over for players to relax somewhat and enjoy their off-season period, which in our case lasts six to eight weeks. This is an opportunity to enjoy liberties that are normally never considered, because they are seen as detrimental to preparation, such as alcohol and junk food. In October 2011, after playing in the AFL Grand Final, I fell into a routine of eating unhealthily and having consecutive late nights partying. There is certainly nothing wrong with enjoying a release from the constant focus and pressure that comes with elite sport and that is what I was doing.

I stopped meditating after the 2011 Grand Final because I fell out of my routine. I knew how beneficial it had been for me and how integral its role was in helping me achieve a still mind, however I felt a great sense of freedom from not being in my normal professional footballer's routine and I did not feel that it was necessary. I felt in total control.

After the fun of having no commitments and being on holiday for six weeks, it was time to return to preseason training. Preseason training is very difficult. The physical nature of AFL football means players are required to have an elite all-round fitness that combines strength, endurance and power. To achieve the right balance for the sport, training can be gruelling at times, particularly during the first stages of preseason. I had not meditated at all throughout the entire six-week break. I was aware of this, however felt perfectly comfortable with my mental state.

When I commenced training, I decided to try to get back into my routine of meditation, but found it extremely hard to concentrate when I sat down and closed my eyes. I could not keep still and my mind was racing with so many thoughts. It was extremely uncomfortable, so I would stop after five minutes of trying. This occurred a handful of times during the first week of training. I could not get into it and kept telling myself that it didn't matter if I missed meditating, because I was perfectly fine. After a few more unsuccessful attempts, I was into a routine of not even trying to do it and, after a while, I completely stopped thinking about the importance of having a still mind.

Often, when we reach a satisfactory level in anything through our deliberate efforts, we forget exactly what it took to get there. This is precisely what happened to me. Through deliberate effort, I had been able to overcome the many troubles in my life. When I looked back on how I was able to achieve this, and still function stress-free, I felt as though I was bulletproof. Even when I had stopped using meditation to achieve a calm mind, I still felt the effects of the hard work that I had put in, and this made me complacent. If any individual were to begin a rigorous daily exercise regime for a couple of months and achieve significant improvements with their fitness, they would still feel the benefits of the regime for some weeks after they stopped exercising. But the longer that they remained completely without exercise, the more their fitness levels would continue to diminish, until one day they would find that their fitness was back to where it was before they started the regime. This is what occurred with me. My still mind became unstable very quickly.

After completing our first phase of preseason training in late 2011, from the start of November through to Christmas, it was time for us to enjoy our Christmas break. By this stage I had fallen out of my meditation routine, but still felt perfectly fine and was getting through life relatively stress-free. I was extremely excited because, on Christmas Eve, I had booked to fly out of Melbourne to spend my two-week holiday in Rio de Janeiro, relaxing with family and friends. I landed in Rio about 8pm and headed straight for my Aunty's apartment, where many family members were awaiting my arrival.

In Brazil, Christmas tradition is for presents to be exchanged at midnight on Christmas Eve. I felt like Santa Claus, with my suitcase full of presents to exchange with my family and friends. After sharing a delicious Christmas dinner, playing and dancing to samba music, it was midnight—time to exchange gifts with one another. We all shared in the joy that Christmas brings and I felt a great sense of bliss.

After the two-week holiday, I arrived back in Melbourne to commence the final phase of preseason training. I had thoroughly enjoyed my holidays in Rio, where I was able to feel as though I had become part of a reality that was extremely foreign to the one I experience in Australia. Getting back into training was extremely difficult. I was able to meet the requirements physically; however I was really struggling to keep up mentally. Initially I found that I had an enormous lack of motivation to want to train. I began to think a lot more about my childhood, the suicide of my stepfather and the debts he left behind, and other traumatic experiences my family and I had endured recently.

My mind would often be flooded with thoughts that I could not control. It would engage in its own dialogue, which made it very hard for me to concentrate when I was at my football club. I knew that I did not feel this way before, when I had had much more stillness in my mind. Eventually the constant noise of my mind became the norm and I stopped worrying that I could not calm it down. It just felt normal to be sitting in my car, stressing about the bills I had to pay and the things I had forgotten to do. If it wasn't the future that I was stressing about it was my past; the things I should have done or had missed out on.

After a while I began getting frustrated easily. It took very little to set me off. One time I was driving and a man cut me off. I made sure I sped up to be alongside him, tooted my horn and swore at him as aggressively as I could. I knew that I was not like this before and started to realise that I had lost a lot of control over my mind. My mind would tick over until I just wanted it to stop, and the only way to do that was to keep my mind active by watching television or going on my phone and opening up Facebook or Twitter.

Early days in Melbourne, Australia: 3 years old.

Vila Isabel, Rio de Janeiro: Playing in our
family courtyard 'concrete jungle'.

Always knew relaxation was important!

Hanging out on the stairs as a 4 year old.

Year 1 of primary school – Templestowe, Victoria.

Trying to steer the ship in the right direction.

First day of school: Eltham Primary School.

Under 9's Gold medal 4x100, Western Australian
state relay championships.

Little athletics really broadened my horizons as
an athlete, teaching me to apply myself to
a range of disciplines.

In Black and White colours – Rossmoyne Under 11's. With my long time junior teammate and friend, Trent Ovens

Jongo da Serrinha – Traditional Afro-Brazilian spiritual dance. This culture is very dear to my heart.

New Years Eve, Rio de Janeiro. Wearing the traditional white,
as everyone does, to symbolise new beginnings.

A child's laughter = true bliss

Matthew, me, Gabriel and Raquel

On top of the mountain and flying the flag.

Football starting to get more serious – 14 years old.

Collingwood Best and Fairest night, 2008. Raquel,
Ralph (my step father) and my Mum made it
across the country to be there and support.

Celebrating a crucial goal against Sydney in honour
of my friend: RIP 'Marreta'.

Focused to make the play count!

In a state of Nirvana after scoring a goal
in the 2010 Grand Final win.

In the powerful presence of His Holiness the Dalai Lama, 2011.

The motivation to get up in the morning and go to training became weaker and weaker. I began to take more notice of people complaining about things I considered petty and insignificant. I started to feel extremely isolated and alone at my football club, which is where I spent the majority of my time. I felt as though no-one could truly understand the experiences I had gone through in the last three years and that I had no-one to turn to. That is when I began to resent going to my football club.

The unresolved anger and frustration that I felt inside began to express itself through the people I was closest to in my life—my family. I would find myself getting into arguments with my mother about my past and worries for the future. I would engage my mother in conversations about my stepfather and tell her that I had absolutely no respect for him. I would say to her, 'He was a f---ing coward. He tormented my childhood then left a mess behind so we all had to pick up the pieces.' Mum would not respond to me in a defensive manner, because she knew full well that would make me angrier. She would just say, 'I think you need to speak to someone, Heritier. You have a lot of hate built up inside of you that you need to resolve.' She said it in a calm manner, however I would still get angry at her assessment of me and would say to her, 'You have to face reality; he was a f---ing prick and he f---ed our lives up.' Mum remained silent and I could tell that she was hurting inside. This made me feel as though I had won.

As the weeks of preseason training passed, I began to find it harder and harder to get out of bed. I would be woken by my alarm, but when I tried to get out of bed I just couldn't. I would just stare at my phone and see the minutes ticking along. Before I knew it, 30 minutes had passed and I still couldn't move. I eventually willed myself to get out of bed to go to training, but I would now be running late. The first few times I arrived late it was swept under the carpet, because it was so out of character for me and everyone accepted it as being just a mistake. My coach, Nathan Buckley, asked me if there was something going on and I told him that I was fine. He would respond by telling me to make sure it did not happen again. Sometimes I would arrive late and manage to sneak in without anybody noticing. After arriving so late one day that my team were already out on the training grounds, my coach took a much harder line and said, 'Harry, you are a leader of this club and arriving late is just not good enough. I have given you the benefit of the doubt a few times now, but you have not changed. This is a big concern.' I agreed with him and told him I was deeply sorry and that it would not happen again.

I did not want to feel the way I was feeling. I hated the fact that my life was not running as smoothly as it should have been. I kept comparing how I felt in the past while in the midst of grieving the loss of my dad to how I was currently feeling, which was a whole lot worse. I felt terrible—not only at football, but in my entire life. I saw myself as a failure and would constantly think about how I had made so many mistakes. I did not want to leave my house at all. Friends would invite me to go out for dinner or to catch up for a coffee, but I did not have enough energy and would rather sit at home alone in my own cave of thoughts than engage with people. I wished that I could have gone and enjoyed myself socially; however I knew that I was not feeling normal and that made me experience great anxiety.

One day I decided to go out with my older brother Gabriel and some friends. I thought it would be a great opportunity to relax and take my mind off all the stress I was experiencing. It was a Sunday, with perfect summer weather. There was a strict policy that players not consume alcohol on the day prior to a training session. However, I took the liberty of ignoring that rule and justified doing so through my current state of mind. I began drinking early on in the day from around midday. I felt great at the time and was really enjoying the company of friends. I remember reflecting on how that was the way life was meant to be. My mind was not noisy and I felt completely relaxed. I continued to drink all through the day in the sun and was quite intoxicated by late afternoon. Conscious of the fact that I had training the next day, my brother Gabriel told me to go home and rest up. He took me out onto the street and hailed a cab for me.

When I reached home, I saw Mum and began to have a conversation with her. I began to speak about my stepfather and told her exactly what I felt about him at the time. I was harbouring a lot of pain inside me that I had carried for a few years and it was all about to come out. Mum couldn't do anything about it. She tried her best to keep silent. But the more she did, the angrier I became. I then went through my entire childhood and brought up everything that was left unresolved: from how tormented I had felt about my stepfather, to how I never felt as though I belonged to my family. Mum cracked and began to cry and that is when I began to throw things around the house in anger. 'I am f---ing sick of all this shit. I am 25 years old and I do not need all of this f---ing responsibility! That prick that was your husband f---ed up all of our lives!'

Mum moved in to her room and that is when I followed her in to continue my barrage of hateful words. I told her that I was sick and tired of life and that is when I punched the tall mirror attached to her antique clothes cabinet. The mirror shattered, but I continued to punch hole after hole into the cabinet. When I realised that my fist was bleeding badly, I began to kick the cabinet, putting more holes into it. By the end of my rage, there were hundreds of pieces of shattered mirror and trails of blood everywhere. I looked down at my fist and shin which were both bleeding profusely. I noticed that my knuckles had jagged bits of mirror inside them. I looked at my mother who was so terrified that she was curled up in a corner of the room, shaking. I made eye contact with her, and then went into the bathroom to wash my cuts. I pulled many bits of mirror out of my fist and put it under a running tap. I noticed how much of a mess I had made of my hand. I turned off the tap and wrapped my hand completely with toilet paper. I began to feel the throbbing pain of my cuts and went and lay down on my bed. My head began to spin and my heart was still beating from my episode of rage. I remember being scared of myself because the thoughts that were going through my head were of suicide. I told myself that my life was not worth living and I just wanted the pain to all end. I began to cry and wish that I could just go back to when life was so much simpler. All the intense emotion I was feeling began to tire me out and that is when I fell asleep.

I woke up early in the morning, well before my alarm. As I rolled over to reach for my phone to see what time it was, I felt an immediate pain in my hand. I looked at my hand, which was wrapped in toilet paper and soaked with blood, and remembered all that had occurred the night before. I felt enormous shame and guilt for my actions. I thought about how my mum must have felt and began to feel a wave of sadness wash over my body. I got up and decided to see what my hand looked like. I went to the bathroom to unwrap the bloodied toilet paper from my hand—it made it resemble that of a mummy. I unravelled the toilet paper centimetre by centimetre, as the blood had dried so was stuck to my wound. I decided that it would be best to wet the toilet paper first, to make it a little easier and less painful to pull off. I put my hand under the running tap and bit by bit removed the toilet paper until the wounds were revealed. There were many cuts all over my fist, but the biggest cut was on the knuckle of my pinky finger. It was a deep jagged cut that looked disgusting. There were still pieces of glass lodged in the finger which I tried in vain to remove because the pain was too great. I decided to leave my hand as it was and take a shower. I could smell the alcohol oozing out of my pores, so it felt good to wash myself up.

After my shower, I thought it would be best to get ready to go to my football club. The medical staff are always the first to arrive at the club and I knew I had to see someone immediately about my hand. I got changed, then hopped into my car and drove off to the club with one hand. When I arrived, there were a few players and coaches already there. I did not want anyone to see my hand, so I slid it into my jeans pocket as best as I could, trying not to rub my wounds, a difficult and painful task. I made an effort to walk inside as inconspicuously as I could to avoid contact with anyone and headed for the doctor's room. A coach saw me walking through the corridors and called out to me to stop for a chat. He asked me questions about my weekend and what I had got up to. I answered and made small talk with him so he was not suspicious. Then I made my way to the doctor's room.

I knocked on his door and walked in to find the doctor sitting at his desk typing away at his computer then said, 'Doc, I f---ed up.' I pulled my hand out of my jeans pocket and grimaced with pain as the wound scraped against the denim. Before he could respond by asking me what I meant, my hand was dangling in front of his face. 'Oh s--t' he said, and shut the door behind me. 'Take a seat,' he said. I told him exactly what had happened: that I was going through a tough time and had put my hand through a mirror in anger. He was completely non-judgemental. 'I'm here to help you,' he said in a calm voice. He told me that my hand needed stitches; but because I had waited overnight, it was too late to get it done. After cleaning my wounds he decided that it would be best to put in a couple of stitches, just to clamp the wound together. After stitching me up, he told me to go home immediately and not to worry about telling the coaches as he would advise them that I was at home. 'Just go home and clear your head,' he said. I thanked him for his help then left the club, feeling a great sense of shame.

On the drive back home, I kept thinking about Mum and how she must have been feeling. The shame continued to grow and grow so I went and lay in bed and fell asleep soon after. I was awoken from my slumber by my phone ringing. It was my coach, Nathan Buckley. My heart started beating rapidly when I saw his name come up and I tried to keep as composed as possible when I answered the phone. The first thing he asked me was if I was okay. I told him that I was going through a few things and that I needed help to get through them. The conversation was short and he told me that he would see me when I was in the club next.

During the rest of that day I realised how I really did need to get some help, because I had lost control. The new injury that I had sustained ruled me out of our first preseason game to be played that weekend. But that was the least of my worries. I was once a person who was calm and able to stay composed when under stress or adversity. Now I realised the danger I faced if I did not do something to get on top of my mental state.

The next morning I arrived early at the football club to see my coach, Nathan Buckley. As soon as I walked into his office, I told him I was sorry and explained that I was going through a really tough time. He told me that, whatever I needed, he and the club were there for me. I became emotional and began to tell him how I felt. He said that I needed to do whatever I could to ensure I could recover, and I knew immediately that was to admit that I needed professional help. Before I left his office, he told me to walk over to him. He looked me in the eyes and opened his arms indicating he wanted me to give him a hug. After that moment I knew that I had a lot of work to do to myself and that I had to start immediately.

I walked out of Nathan's office and straight into the office of the club's head of psychological services, and told him that I needed to see a psychologist. He told me he had already sensed that something was not right with me prior to that moment, due to my uncharacteristic lateness and what he described as my lack of motivation and passion. I refuted his observations to begin with. However the more he continued to enquire about my wellbeing, the more I opened up to him. Initially, I told him that I was working through a few things and was capable of doing so alone. He recommended that I see a psychologist; but the thought of seeing a 'shrink' made me quiver inside. I thought to myself that I didn't need the help of someone else and that I could battle through this phase myself. Now I was in his office I realised that I needed to make a change and there was no shame in getting some help along the way. I had become so accustomed to helping people when they were down that I had begun to believe that I was immune to receiving 'help' myself. 'I need to see someone,' I said to him. Without judgment or even asking for specific information, he responded by saying he would do anything and everything possible to help me out.

People say that *There is no shame in getting help.* However based on my experiences I disagree, because the thing you must break through in most cases is the shame you feel for thinking you are inferior or incapable of sorting out your own life. Within a few days of the meeting at the club, I attended my first appointment with my new psychologist. He told me that I had experienced enough trauma in my life to trigger my depression and anxiety. He explained how both are thought disorders and that, with work, they can be overcome. He asked me if I had ever looked into meditation. I told him that I had once meditated regularly, and that it had helped me to experience calmness and serenity, but I had got out of the routine. I immediately knew that I needed to start meditating again and that was reaffirmed by my psychologist's response, 'I think you should get back into that routine.'

Meditation was not the 'cure' for stabilising my mind, but it certainly fast-tracked the recovery process of my mental health. After numerous sessions with the psychologist, I began to work through some of the deepest and darkest things that I had experienced but never addressed. What tends to happen when we face trauma or tragedy is that we acknowledge that they have occurred, however over time we lock them away and never take ourselves back to those moments to learn and grow from what they have to offer. You may be thinking about an experience that you have had in your life that you have not spoken to anyone about and be thinking, 'That's bulls--t! How on earth am I going to learn and grow from … ' The truth is, I do not have the answer to that. However, you will be surprised by how things that you've pushed to the back of your mind—that you always knew existed but did not acknowledge—can come back to haunt you later on in your life. That is exactly what happened to me.

During the period of my life where I lost my stepfather to suicide and went through financial loss, I was able to keep the storm at bay, so to speak, through regular meditation. However, there was a missing ingredient. Meditation allowed me to feel calm while still knowing that there was a lot of s--t going on in the background. I had not faced reality, and what I mean by that is that I had not spoken to anyone about my challenges. Of course people would ask how I was and I would reply. However, it is very easy to have a conversation that lies on the surface. For example:

THEM: Harry, how is everything going? I know you must be going through a tough time.

ME: Yes, it is tough and I have my moments, but each day I grow more strength.

THEM: You are such a strong person and I just want to let you know I'm here for you.

ME: Thank you so much, I know I can always count on you. You are an amazing friend and I am so grateful to have you in my life.

This is a typical conversation that I would have with the people around me. Sometimes it would be more in-depth than this, but I never really got deep enough to reveal exactly how I was feeling at the time. And even if I were to reveal how I was really feeling, unless the person were a psychologist/psychiatrist, they would not have been able to give me a response or a strategy to effectively and efficiently move forward. Psychologists and psychiatrists have acquired specific knowledge and understanding through years of deliberate study and practice. No matter how good the intentions of the people in my life that I would converse with in regards to my mental state, they were not equipped with empirical understanding of what was the best way forward for me.

This is a mistake that most of us make. We think that 'help' is not for us because the word 'help' carries such negative connotations in relation to mental health. This is the mistake that I made. However after realising that I could potentially harm myself through the suicidal thoughts I was having, I decided to do something different from what I was currently doing. If you keep on doing what you have always done you will get the same results and the same results for me meant self-harm, deeper depression and anxiety.

My psychologist spoke to me in an objective manner. He had no emotional ties to my life and used his expertise to assist and guide me beyond my mental turmoil. Sometimes after the sessions, I would feel emotionally drained, because he would take me back to times and places that I had pushed to the back of my mind but that still affected me. He got to the root of my issues by listening attentively and asking specific questions that allowed me to contemplate what was going on in my life. At times it was really difficult, because I had never really had to take myself back to those times emotionally. When you completely take yourself back to dark moments, it is as though you are reliving them, something that I never considered or intended to do ever again. However what my psychologist was able to do was take me back to the roots of these traumas and change my perspective on how I could see and live with them in my future. Each time I went through an issue, I would come out the other end with a completely new perception of the issue. The issues were no longer forced to the back to be somewhat blocked out in my mind. I now acknowledged the issueshad occurred, however my entire perception had shifted. So I was now comfortable about continuing my life, knowing I had closed that chapter in my life.

We live in a subjective world: we give meaning to everything that is happing to us or around us. Every one of us will experience tragedy and adversity in our lives, in some way, shape or form. Some of us are able to push through tragedy and trauma seemingly unscathed, and I was one of those people. However the conclusion that I have come to now is that a situation that may seem to be in control can quite easily be triggered off the rails by something totally unrelated. Sometimes the catalyst for a downward spiral can be one of the smallest things. The best quote I know in relation to this is: *The straw that broke the camel's back*.

Be proactive with your mental health and the divine nature of our reality will open up to you. What I mean by this is that, once you address the issues that have caused you much pain and suffering, you will be transformed.

Don't wait, like I did, for the effects to hit you again in the future or hold you back in the present. Address them as soon as possible.

When you're not in the arena, it suggests you don't have much control; that there are fewer things that you **can** control in your life than you **can't** control. You can control minor things, for example small daily actions, like brushing your teeth and driving your car. However, bigger things that require more energy are out of your control. Now that's the ordinary day-to-day mentality. Again, those people who strive to be active in the arena are those who realise that, whatever life's purpose is or whatever journey or path they choose, it has actually been their choice and they are successful in doing so. When asked, 'What if you could control your own life?' a lot of people think straight away: financial wealth, financial gain. Well, no doubt you can control that in your life. But, as you begin playing with your divinity, you will see that there is a whole lot more to life than financial gain. This is only one facet of feeling the sweet soil of the arena beneath your feet.

THE 3-STEP CONSCIOUS CREATION PROCESS

Now I will introduce you to a methodology, which I have gained through empirical understanding, direct experience and observation of times when I have succeeded in manifesting, Consciously creating, and watching other people being successful and unsuccessful. I have formulated a process, based on my observation of how things are Consciously created. It's called the 3-Step Conscious Creation Process.

Obviously, there is a whole lot more to the creation process than three steps. It would be stupid to suggest that there are only three steps that you need to follow to create something. Life and creation are far more complex than our minds can comprehend. But it's important to have guidelines, because guidelines are things that you can use as a reference point to know that you are in the right direction and to help develop your own formula. This formula that I will introduce to you is not something that I have made up; it's not something that I have invented. It has come from the many 'greats' and 'not so greats' that I have observed before me. They have followed and understood the creation process, and they've Consciously created; whether Nelson Mandela, Barack Obama or Princess Diana. The greats in history have shown us how to Consciously create, how to follow our own life's purpose in a successful and efficient manner. Of course, they've had their downfalls. Of course, they've failed. I don't remember who told me exactly, it may have been one of my coaches, that there's no harm in failing if it's in the pursuit of success. And while the people who I have just mentioned may have either failed or had downfalls, they've Consciously created their intended outcome to be successful.

I like to use an analogy to show why it is important to follow a simple process, so that you understand how the creation process works. Like I said, it would be stupid to suggest that the creation process is as simple as three steps. However, the analogy that I use is based on the understanding that most of us have about how to plant a seed—literally, plant a seed.

We all know how flowers grow: you must have a seed, you put it below fertile soil, and you water it. If you water it enough and it has plenty of sun, then you know that the seed will germinate and a beautiful flower will appear above the surface of the soil. Continue to water, and it will grow. And there you have it: a flower will blossom out of nowhere—literally a miracle—you're playing God. Now that is my basic understanding of the creation process of a flower. That is my basic understanding of the work of a gardener.

I'm not a gardener, and I don't have the scientific knowledge of how that flower was able to blossom or how that plant was able to break the surface. But I know that the process is very simple, a simple process that I can use. I can go down to my local flower shop and I can buy some seeds and undertake this simple process, knowing full well that there is a chance something will arise from it. There's a chance I might not be successful; I might not be diligent and I might not understand which soil or fertilizer I need to use to create the best environment. However, in time, if I continue on with this process, I will gain an understanding for myself. If I am interested in this, I will continue to ask experts or read magazines; I will do research on the internet; and eventually I will put the pieces of the puzzle together and use a process which is most effective for my own strengths and weaknesses.

Now, from this simple understanding, I can plant a seed and give a beautiful rose to my mother. I may not be able to explain to her the intricacies of the process. But with more research or experience, I might be able to do such a thing. But it's not necessary—it's not necessary at all. I can admit that I might fail; I might not be able to produce these flowers because of inconsistencies in the process. But as long as I have a general idea, that's okay.

The same can be said for the creation process in your own life. Whether you are trying to create or become something, or whether you are trying to manifest something, the same can be said. This is why I am going to introduce you to the three steps in the Conscious creation process. This is a simple process that you can use to gain an understanding for yourself, in order to Consciously create.

STEP 1: IDEA

The first phase of the Conscious creation process is the notion that everything starts off as an idea. To illustrate this, I want you to look around the room you're in now. Find the first thing that is made by a human being. It might be a television. Now take that television, for example. Before the first television was ever created in the physical form, where did it exist? That's a good question to contemplate. Now when you think about it, it did exist before it existed in physical form. It existed as an idea in someone's head! So it existed in a non-physical form in the non-physical realm of someone's head. That person was able to get that concept or that idea from the non-physical realm and manifest it in the physical realm. That's Conscious creation; that is the creation process. The first step is that everything starts off as an idea.

STEP 2: PURPOSE

The second phase of the Conscious creation process is purpose. Purpose is absolutely crucial in the Conscious creation process. Because once you have the idea, it will continue to remain in the non-physical realm if you don't act on it. But it's not as simple as just going from an idea to action. The thing that links them is a *purpose*. Now a purpose is crucial, because it allows you to surpass any pain that might be involved in reaching what you desire. When you are able to identify a purpose, that purpose is the foundation for you. A purpose is the fuel that allows you to drive the vehicle to wherever you'd like to drive it.

An example of purpose that I love using whenever I speak to people, especially young people, is: 'If I were to say to you right now, come and join me for a twenty kilometre run in the clothes you are in, would you do it?' A lot of people look at me and say, 'Of course not.' I would then say, 'Put your hands up' and a lot of you would probably think I was crazy if I asked you to do that. Twenty kilometres is a long way. You may even run marathons; you may even be a long distance runner. But if you were to do it right now you would not be prepared, because you know that there is a lot of pain attached to those twenty kilometres. So you wouldn't do it. But what if I was to say to you: 'In the clothes you are in right now, you've got to run with me for twenty kilometres. And at the end of those twenty kilometres, there will be twenty million dollars waiting for you.' Now how many would say 'yes'? You see the power of purpose? You see how purpose can surpass pain? Amazing isn't it!

Purpose has been the very thing that has led history's greats to enjoy the greatest of pain. A lot of us look back in observation and think, 'Gee, how did that person do that?' It's because they're connected to their purpose, the purpose to fuel the creation process. Purpose led Nelson Mandela to survive in a prison cell for 27 years and then come out and changed the whole nation, arguably changing the whole world and how we relate to each other. Purpose allowed Aron Ralston, an extreme adventure seeker on whom the film *127 Hours* was based, to cut off his own arm—to mutilate his own arm in order to survive. You think, 'Geez, I couldn't do that, cut off my own arm. No way would I be able to do that.' Well Ralston said, 'Trust me you could.' If your purpose was to live, then you could do it. That's what got him through: the will to live. Purpose allowed him to surpass the physical pain of cutting off his own arm. Phenomenal!

The same could be used for any process. But a lot of people get it wrong, because they don't stay connected to their purpose. Purpose allows you to surpass pain. Yes, you might say it will still hurt, but when you have a purpose you will continue on. Now, a lot of people are ineffective in Consciously creating their lives because they don't understand that, in the creation process, purpose is essential. So they have an idea and they try to act on that idea straight away, without identifying a purpose and reminding themselves to stay connected to that purpose. What happens is, in the first few days, they go 'Okay.' But then that commitment just drops away, and they fall into procrastination.

A perfect example of this would be someone who is trying to follow a stringent diet. It's a New Year's resolution to lose ten kilos, just for their general health and wellbeing. They know they have to lose weight, and they decide that they want to go ahead and act on it. They are all enthusiastic, 'Yes! I'm going to look good. I'm going to lose weight.' They even get a pair of brand new running shoes as a Christmas gift from a family member, so they can start running. 'Yes! I'm going to start running every day or every second day.'

As the new year begins, they put on their new runners and take off into the world. They run on the first day for twenty minutes. They feel great about themselves and they are breaking a sweat. After the run, they arrive back home and they feel fantastic; they feel a sense of fulfilment, 'Yes, I'm running.' On the second day that they are intending to run they do run, but this time they start getting a little bit sore and tired. They run for about fifteen minutes and they think, 'Well look, I've run today. Fifteen minutes isn't twenty minutes, but it's still good! I'm still running. I'll stop now.' So they go home still feeling good about themselves. They did something. The five minutes they cut off is insignificant. They next day they are scheduled to run and the same applies. They run for about ten minutes and they think, 'Gee, I'm tired. But I've run twice before this. This is my third time. I'm still going okay. I've gone from nothing to this. I'll settle.' And they decide to stop and go home.

The next day that they schedule to run, a friend comes over unexpectedly with a few beers, or with some other

IT'S COOL TO BE CONSCIOUS

form of distraction. 'Come on, let's go out.' And that person knows that they've got a schedule; they know that they want to lose weight. But the allure of that other pleasure is far outweighing. They make the concession for themselves. They've already run three times before, so they can just let this one slip. They decide to go with their friend and take the easy option. Then, the next time that they are scheduled to run, they don't even think about it. They fall into the same rut that they had been stuck in. They say that they will run next time, which is the foundation for procrastination.

The foundation for procrastination is a lack of purpose. Purpose allows you to surpass pain. If that person had stayed connected to the purpose, then they would have continued on.

An example of how the same person could have stayed connected to that purpose is: when purpose is thrust upon you, then you are forced to act. You are always reminded of that purpose. Let's look at it this way. What if that same person who was losing weight for their health and wellbeing didn't personally make the decision, but was told by their physician that if they didn't lose 10 to 15 kilos of weight they would be at a greater risk of heart disease, which could lead to an early death in a short period of time? For a lot of people, that is a purpose thrust upon them. They have to choose whether or not to live or die. It could be the difference between living an extra ten years or dying a lot sooner. A lot of people would take action straight away. They would decide, 'Okay, I'm going to start running' and they would! Every day they'd wake up and

- 68 -

they'd be reminded of it. They'd look in the mirror and they'd think, 'If I do not lose this weight, I could die in a short amount of time. I could lose everything, including my family and my friends; everything!' So they stay connected to their purpose. And that purpose allows them to surpass the pain they felt about running. They might have a friend come over and offer distractions, but they connect to that purpose and remind themselves why they're doing it. That is the power of purpose.

You can see examples of purpose in your everyday life, whether it is someone who has a health scare or whether it is someone who is told that they'll lose their job, if they don't increase their performance at work. Such people have purpose thrust upon them.

Here's my question: why wait until purpose is thrust upon you? Without purpose, you will procrastinate. Purpose is a key ingredient in the creation process. Purpose is powerful. Stay connected to your purpose and you will be able to move mountains.

STEP 3: ACTION

The third phase of the Conscious creation process is action. It's one thing to see the path. You have your idea and you have your purpose, so the next phase is to take action and walk that path. And yes, part of action is also failing.

Action can be put into place once you have decided to make changes. With your newly-found purpose supporting you, possibilities will begin to surround you. Louise L. Hay provides us with invaluable information in her book, *The Power Is Within You*. Louise writes:

There is a lot of information available that will give you ideas once you are willing to change; it is remarkable how the Universe begins to help you. It brings you what you need. It could be a book, a tape, a teacher or even a friend making a passing remark that suddenly has deep meaning to you.

Keeping what Louise said in mind will encourage you to be more aware of your surroundings, and you'll be more open to the infinite possibilities that are a part of your everyday life. The key to taking action and to begin creating what you really want in life is to observe, be aware and make use of what's already in front of you. By doing this, action is already taking place.

It's so easy to consume information, ideas and the wisdom of others and this is great to get us motivated, but we need to take action and apply it to our lives.

My sister Raquel provided a great example of 'taking action' when she took a year off from her studies in order to save up as much money as possible. She was keen to travel to Brazil and stay there for over six months. I observed with keen interest how she dedicated herself to working extremely hard at two jobs. She had a goal in mind, so wouldn't let anything get in her way, even minimal sleep. She had her target and would not stop until she had met it. Raquel managed to save up what she thought was enough money to buy her plane tickets, accommodation and have enough spending money for the whole time she planned to spend in Brazil. She budgeted well, so was confident that she would be able to be comfortable on her travels.

When Raquel arrived in Rio de Janeiro, she was over-whelmed with excitement. The colours, language, smells and sounds were all new to her. She told me at the time that, early on in her trip, she was just so happy from the satisfaction of knowing that she was the one responsible for creating her experiences herself: 'I have worked so hard and sacrificed so much through the course of a year, and now I'm seeing the rewards!'

Over the months Raquel was gone, I kept up-to-date with her travels through her constant Facebook posts and regular Skype conversations. She was having the time of her life.

About four and a half months into her trip, Raquel sent me an email telling me that she needed to speak to me urgently. I was quite worried, so I called her right away. To my relief Raquel was fine, although there was something troubling her. That was when she told me that her money was running out.

She was very upset with herself, because she had spent a little more than she had planned. She told me that she did not want to have to come back from her travels early. I asked her what she intended doing and she said that she would try to find a job. She then told me that it would be very difficult, because she still had some difficulty speaking Portuguese. She was frustrated by the thought of not being able to find work and having to return to Australia because of a lack of funds.

I could sense her frustration and told her that she was actually in a very exciting situation and I was jealous! I told her that, no matter what, she would never starve to death, because she was fortunate enough to have many people in her life who would never allow such a thing to happen. I then told her that, if she really wanted to, she could create her own destiny herself. I reminded her of the importance of following the process of creation and that she could get started right away. 'What are you going to do about it Raquel?' I asked.

Raquel told me that she would get started right away. Her first step was to identify that she could get a job and that speaking English would work in her favour. She had her mind set on working in hospitality, because she believed that she'd be able to fast-track her Portuguese through the interaction it required. Her next step was to create a CV in Portuguese. Fortunately, a cousin was happy to assist her with this task. I reminded her of the important final step of action: to make sure she did not give up after the first few hurdles.

After that phone conversation, I could tell that she was very inspired and was ready to create her own opportunities. I called her after a couple of days just to touch base. She told me that she had already made her CV and intended to meet with the manager of every restaurant and bar, to personally deliver it to them. I was impressed and also excited to hear about how her mission was going.

After a few more days, Raquel called me with some exciting news. She had landed herself a job in one of Rio de Janeiro's most upmarket restaurants. She told me that the manager had been impressed by her courage and determination to find herself a job. He told her that these two qualities would ensure that her limitations could easily be overcome.

As it turned out, Raquel spent a further three months in Rio de Janeiro, earning more than three times the salary of most people her age. She had more than enough money to be comfortable and her Portuguese became fluent, because of her working environment. She made such an impact in her place of work through her courage and determination that, when she decided that it was time to return to Australia to resume her studies, her boss begged her to stay. He told her that, from day one, he had been so impressed by her that he knew he was losing a very valuable employee. He even offered her a considerable bonus.

As she walked out of the restaurant on her last day of work, she was approached by two more restaurant owners who had heard about this courageous and determined woman who had become invaluable. They also offered her jobs at their restaurants which she graciously refused, because her time in Brazil was coming to an end.

After reflecting on Raquel's story, you may begin to compare it to situations where you have or have not decided to Consciously create your own life. There may be some of you who think: 'This would never happen to me; she is just a lucky girl.' Well, of course it will never happen to you, if you continue to think that way.

I love this story and it often inspires and reminds me that we really do have the power.

The thing that most impresses and inspires me is the fact that Raquel took action and did not stop at the first 'no'. She handed in her CV to more than 30 different places, because she knew that the harder you try, the more likely you are to stay in the game.

Now I'm sure you'll agree that the three stepping stones to Consciously creating form a simple process, one that can be followed by anyone who is looking to create what they desire in their lives.

CONSCIOUS TIPS TO REMEMBER

- If you want to wake up each morning smiling and knowing you're making the world a better place, start by following your passion.

- You have a choice to either hang on to negative feelings, or dropkick them and let them go.

- Finding your passion will help you to feel completely Conscious and in the moment. You will experience a new sense of liberation.

- There are endless ways in which you can express yourself. If your passion is music, think about all the elements that make up the industry and see where you would fit best.

- Consciously think about what it is that you love to do, and your passions will start to flow.

- Rethink your current feelings surrounding intelligence by reflecting on Dr Gardner's eight categories. Where do you see yourself?

- Always stick to what you want to do, not what other believe you should be doing.

- The Conscious creation process is crucial to manifesting your ideas into reality. You can absolutely control and create far more than you think.

- Make an effort to learn the 3-step Conscious creation process:
  1. Everything starts off as an *idea*
  2. The idea must have *purpose*
  3. Take *action* to transform your idea into reality

- Never limit yourself, because anything is possible.

FOREWORD by the Dalai Lama:

Generating a sense of equanimity is necessary to regulate our fluctuating emotions towards others.

It is very helpful to visualise three people in front of you: one who is your relative or friend, another who is an enemy, and someone towards whom you feel neutral. Observe your natural reaction to them. When you think about your friend, you feel close to her and immediately have a sense of concern for her welfare. When you think about your enemy, you immediately feel uncomfortable and ill at ease. When you think about the person towards whom you feel neutral, you find you do not really care whether that person is miserable or happy.

Your friend has not always been your friend, and your enemy has not always been hostile. Therefore, it is foolish to be only concerned with those we think of now as friends and to disregard those we think of as enemies.

PILLAR 3:
BECOME MORE OBSERVANT AND LABEL CONSCIOUS

> *Judgements prevent us from seeing*
> *the good that lies beyond appearances.*
>
> Wayne W. Dyer, self-development guru

The **third pillar** is observing what you take in and being Conscious of labels. Everyone knows that you can't judge a book by its cover. Who would have thought that a skinny Afro-Brazilian boy would one day get paid for kicking a ball between two white poles?

One of the reasons I love talent shows is because they prove my point perfectly. When Susan Boyle came out on stage, if everyone had judged her solely on her appearance, the world would have missed out on an amazing talent. She didn't fit the 'traditional' idea of what a performer should look like and yet, despite her appearance, she had such a beautiful voice to share with the world.

Throughout this chapter, I will address the idea that many of us are using labels, even on people. I have found that this is directly linked to what we take in on a daily basis through what we see, listen to or read. Firstly, I will draw your attention to how important it is to observe what you take in; in order to break down the barriers that are put up by labels, yet consequently go unnoticed. Secondly, I'll share some examples of labels that exist in the world and show how, by Consciously removing them, possibilities and opportunities flow more easily.

OBSERVE WHAT YOU TAKE IN

Observing what you take in is critical to being Conscious. Now I don't just mean observing what you take in nutritionally, even though it is extremely important to your wellbeing, mentally and physically. I'm speaking more in relation to what you take in and what you consume on a philosophical level.

A lot of people don't understand the extent to which the mind operates. Now I'm not suggesting that I am an expert about the extent to which the mind operates. My understanding is that *many* people don't understand. I'm not saying that they don't know how to use their minds; I'm saying that they haven't mastered how to use them to their full capacity.

The mind can actually be the greatest tool to assist us in life. I believe a lot of people use the mind, but they don't know *how* to use the mind, so to speak. It's just like Wi-Fi internet, for example. We all enjoy the benefits of using Wi-Fi internet to help us connect to the rest of the world, wherever we may be. While we don't fully understand how it works, we know how to make it work for us on our phones and with our laptop in a park or cafe. What I encourage you to do is learn how to manipulate the mind, so that it can be most beneficial to you. To do this, you have to understand how the mind operates. This starts by monitoring your thoughts.

How many thoughts do you think you have a day? This is a great question. A lot of people are unaware. In fact, we have 70,000 thoughts a day. 95% of these are subconscious thoughts: thoughts that we are not aware of on a Conscious level. The other 5% are thoughts that we are aware of. For example, the thoughts that I am having right at this moment while writing are Conscious. However, there's always mental activity occurring, thoughts that we are having on a subconscious level where we have no control, or indirect control. Our thoughts shape our reality. The way that we think shapes the way that we see the world.

Many prominent thinkers over the years, including Max Planck, the German physicist who originated quantum theory, have expressed the above idea in various ways, but the one that I find that best sums the concept up is:

When you change the way you look at things, the things you look at change.

This is absolutely true. But how do you change the way you look at things? It's easy in theory. It's easy to say, 'Oh, just stop thinking that way.' However, think about it: 95% of your thoughts are subconscious. So how do you change those subconscious thoughts? The key is the Conscious part; observing what you take in. What you take in shapes the way that you think.

Now this is done over a period of time. However, it is quite easy, once you start to be the observer in your life and see what you take in on a Conscious level, and also observe what you take in on a subconscious level. This involves understanding your environment and the way you place yourself.

One of the easiest ways to start this observational process is to ask the question: *How do you start your day?* A common way for people to start their day goes something like this: they wake up in the morning to the sound of their alarm, they roll out of bed, unhappy to be awake, thinking about work. *Oh no, I've got work!* They might turn on the TV and start watching their usual breakfast show. They might go outside and get the paper to read messages from an external source. Now there is nothing wrong with taking messages from an external source, but again you have to ask the question: *How do you start your day?*

A lot of people take in those morning messages from an external source, whether it is the newspaper, the news on the radio, or reading a news page online. The majority of the media focuses on negativity, reactive rather than proactive (and we will touch on that a bit later on); reacting to negative situations or circumstances, whether it is a murder, an economic crisis, or a war or conflict. Observe the mainstream media that most people take in, and you will notice that it is fuelled by negativity. It's our love of drama, which fuels the demand for this.

Many people start their day reading these negative stories or watching these negative images. Straight away their Conscious decision was to start with something negative. Those negative thoughts or negative images, more often than not, evoke negative emotions, whether it is anger or guilt or hatred. For example, you pick up the newspaper to see that a person was stabbed to death in their sleep. How do you think that makes you feel? For the majority of human beings this would evoke a negative response. 'How the hell did this happen?' they might ask. They might also ask 'What is wrong with this society that we live in?' or 'Gee, the youth are terrible.' If these are the first things you are consuming when you wake up, think about how that influences your day. If you want to control the thoughts in your mind, it is crucial that you observe what you take in.

Since my high school years, I have always been intrigued by the relationship between someone's state of mind and what they experience in the outer world. Clichés such as *dare to dream* or *think positive* are universally recognised and used automatically by people, when they are asked for advice. This is because such phrases hold a truth that we can all easily recognise; yet we don't apply and practise regularly in our own lives. And that truth is in relation to the great power the human mind has.

A genuine curiosity about how I could improve and utilise the full potential of my mind to create the results and life I wanted, set me off onto a journey of discovery through the limitless information available out there. This journey enabled me to gain a basic understanding of how the human mind actually works. I wanted to become fully aware of how I could ensure my mind was working **for** me, rather than **against** me.

Deepak Chopra consistently speaks about the human mind's responsibility, in creating human experience. Through his works, I learnt that the majority of our thoughts are subconscious thoughts, meaning we can't directly control them. They are generally repeated thoughts that literally determine how we see the world. This means that we cannot directly control the way we see the world, because our subconscious mind controls that. The subconscious mind is shaped and developed through our environment and experiences. That is why we universally understand the importance of raising children in loving environments, because our subconscious minds are going through rapid development during early childhood. This is why the link between violent criminals who had violently abusive childhoods is so common.

Think about the very early stage of childhood, when a parent is trying to teach their baby the names of people and objects. They point to the object or person and repeat the name over and over again. For example, 'Daddy, where is Daddy?' A father will continue to repeat that to his baby, knowing that the human mind is like a sponge, particularly in early childhood. The father knows that the more he repeats the word 'Daddy' to his child, while indicating that he is talking about himself, the faster that information will become second nature to the baby, and there will be no doubt what the sound 'Daddy' represents. Over time the word 'Daddy' will trigger off immediate thought associations, in keeping with the baby's programming and environment.

Through our senses, we perceive the world around us; and inside our minds, we interpret what it all means. Understanding this notion means that you can use your mind to create more of what you want in your world.

What I am trying to get at is that we can lose control of creating the world we want very easily, by forgetting this important link between the mind and life. We can lose control by becoming robots in our society and by not utilising or understanding the precious value of the 5% of thoughts that we have direct control over. These are the thoughts that you are Consciously aware of; that ultimately caused the Conscious decision to pick up this book, open it and read the words. This is your Conscious mind, and it should be your greatest friend. However for most of us, it has become our formidable adversary, responsible for making us see limitation and fear in place of opportunity and love.

A very personal and tragic episode in my family was discovering that my sister was seriously abused, between the ages of 12 and 14, by a family member from Brazil who was living with us at the time. Understandably, this terrible experience led to very negative thought patterns for all of us, which we have all had to deal with over time.

I found out about my sister's turmoil on what actually started out to be a great weekend for me. I remember that moment as if it were yesterday. On the Saturday, we had played the Adelaide Crows in the semi final of the 2009 AFL premiership season. At that time, it was the best win

I had ever been involved in. We had come from behind in the dying stages of the match, to win with literally the last kick of the night. In the first half of the match, we didn't look like scoring. We were not getting the ball into our forward half at all, so our forwards were not getting any scoring opportunities.

The night before, I had had a vivid dream involving my stepfather, who had taken his own life just before the beginning of that season. Freakishly, I had dreamt that I was on the MCG playing against the Adelaide Crows, where I had taken a mark from outside 50 metres from goal. The dream was so real. I could hear the roar of the packed MCG; there had to be at least 80,000 fans, all cheering. I looked up to the lights in the stadium, then looked at the goal to calculate if I was in range. I then began to doubt myself and the inner talk commenced, 'You are not capable of kicking this goal; it's too far out for you.' Just as I was beginning to believe these doubts, I saw my stepfather standing right in front of me. In the dream, I knew that he was dead in real life, but he appeared just as he had been. He stood with such pride and a smile came over his face. He then looked at me dead centre in the eyes and said, 'Heritier, believe in yourself, son. You can do it!' With that, I decided not to pass the ball off and went back with full conviction and kicked the goal.

One of the strangest things is that, the next night, I found myself in almost the exact same scenario. I had taken the ball and was just outside what I believed to be my range. I would have to kick the ball at least 55 metres, so straight away doubts began to arise in my mind. However the doubts did not last long because they triggered my memory of the dream I had had the night before. I could see my stepfather's face once again in front of me and I knew straight away that I would go back and kick the ball through the goalposts. And that is exactly what I did. I got enough momentum in my approach and, just as I did in my dream, kicked the ball straight through the middle of the goals. The ball must have travelled 65 metres or so—a lot further than I thought I could kick. The roar of the crowd was deafening and my body seemed to be overtaken by adrenalin when I uncontrollably curled both my hands to make fists and jumped punching the air in unison.

That was the beginning of our resurgence and we pegged our way back bit by bit throughout the game to find ourselves one point down, with less than a minute of play remaining. We somehow managed to surge the ball forward from the centre of the field into our forward line when the umpire's whistle blew. Jack Anthony (a forward who is no longer at the club) was awarded a free kick on a slight angle 30 metres from our goal. It was a relatively easy kick to execute. But with the immense pressure of knowing that we must be in the dying seconds of the game with everything resting on this one kick, Jack must have been trembling with fear and nerves. I remember holding my breath as he began his approach to goal. There was complete silence as no-one uttered a word in that stadium of 80,000 people. Jack struck the ball with dead straight precision and it sailed through the posts for a goal. The crowd roared louder than I had ever heard in my career. The umpire brought the ball back to the centre of the field and we all knew that there must literally be only a couple of seconds to go in the match. I watched as the ball travelled a few metres from a mad scramble of players, all trying to force the ball in the direction of their respective teams. Then, to the relief of us all, the siren sounded in all its glory! I remember being next to my captain, Nick Maxwell, and racing over to embrace him with all of my strength. We hugged and screamed at the top of our lungs, just so grateful we had made a great escape. We had definitely been a part of one of the great wins in the history of AFL finals football. Later we joined the rest of our teammates, who had congregated near the centre of the field, sharing in the ecstasy the result brought us. I felt as though I had reached heaven in that moment.

After shaking hands with our devastated opponents and thanking them for the game, we made our way off the field as one, heading for the change rooms. Once there, we seemed to get another burst of energy and excitement as we embraced and jumped around uncontrollably with joy. At that point in time I can clearly recall thinking, 'After all the pain I have felt throughout this year, I have finally recaptured the spark inside of me thanks to this win. This is the first time since Dad's suicide that I have experienced true happiness.' I had an enormous sense of gratitude and, in that moment. it felt as though all of my stresses had dissolved right before me. I was beginning to see life moving beyond the tragedy that had affected me so deeply.

When I walked out to the car park from the change rooms, I felt as though I was floating on clouds. I was full of optimism and still buzzing with excitement, for our team had progressed through to the next phase of the finals series, placing us two wins away from winning the premiership. As a child, I had always dreamt of winning an AFL Grand Final and holding the cup above my head in a stadium full of screaming fans. My imagination took me back to that time as a child, when life was so simple. I had a daydream about how little I had had to worry about then, other than going to school, doing my homework and, of course, playing sport on the weekends. Now life had become so much more serious. I had moved away from my family to pursue a career as a professional sportsman, I had to cook for myself and pay my own bills, and now I had faced the greatest tragedy of my life through losing my stepfather to suicide. However, winning that final allowed me to connect to my childhood dreams.

For the rest of that night I could not stop smiling or thinking about achieving my childhood dreams of playing in a premiership team. That year I had found it hard to sleep and often stayed awake, thinking about how and why my stepfather had killed himself. That night, however, I slept really well. The feeling of optimism and pure joy seemed to have flowed into the next day because, when I woke up, the first thing I did was lie in bed feeling overwhelming gratitude for a few moments before hopping out of bed. Then I was ready to take on the day with a smile.

My older brother Gabriel had flown over from Perth with his girlfriend Renee to watch the game and was staying at a friend's house. I gave him a call to arrange to meet up at a cafe to have breakfast and enjoy each other's company. It had been a very tough year for all of my family members and he was no exception. He was particularly close to my stepfather and I noticed he still seemed to be in a state of shock. After my stepfather's funeral, I had to return to Melbourne to continue on with my life as a professional footballer. Gabriel could not leave the scene, so to speak, as easily as I could. He was left with my mother to pick up the pieces my stepfather had left behind. This took its toll on him.

When we met at the cafe I could see immediately from Gabriel's eyes that he was also in a state of bliss after watching me play and win. He told me that he was a proud older brother and that all those hours he'd spent roughing me up in the backyard had held me in good stead. To hear him tell me he was proud meant the world to me and increased my feelings of happiness. The day was getting even better! We had ordered our breakfasts and continued to converse in a way full of banter that those who have siblings recognise as a way of expressing affection. Gabriel was midway through telling a joke when all of a sudden my phone began to ring. Gabriel has a magical way of capturing the full attention of those he's speaking to, a pure storyteller. I initially ignored the call because I was so engaged in Gabriel's joke and didn't want to miss the punch-line. But the phone continued to ring, making it hard to ignore, so I looked down to see who it was. I saw it was my mum, so I decided to take the call. I excused myself from the table and moved outside for some privacy.

I answered the call with a very happy 'Hello Mum!' She responded in a less enthusiastic manner, which immediately prompted concern. She said, 'Heritier, I have you on loudspeaker and Raquel is in the room. I have called to tell you that Raquel just told me that, when she was younger, she was raped. Now she does not ...'

That was all I heard; I began to tremble and my knees felt weak. I immediately dropped to the ground in the middle of the street and my legs gave way. My phone followed suit and came crashing to the ground as I released my grip on it. I became crippled by what I had just heard. After a few moments trembling on the ground on my hands and knees I let out a helpless cry, then searched for my phone. My mother was still on the other end of the line, calling my name. I told her that I could not talk and said that I would call her back as soon as I let Gabriel know.

My brother and I developed feelings of extreme hatred towards my sister's abuser, as we contemplated all that we would do to him to avenge her. Although she had buried the memories of the event for years, our dad's death brought all this back to the surface, and made Raquel spiral into a terrible bout of depression. It took her subsequent suicide attempt to make us all realise that something in the way we were all dealing with this event had to change.

Up until this point everyone in my family had been very sympathetic towards Raquel and allowed her the licence to lash out. No-one would ever dare argue with her, for fear that it could lead to an episode of self-destruction. Now I felt that it was time to treat her differently. So many times she had threatened and attempted self-harm and we had all said 'poor girl'. However, that had only brought about the same results. I told Raquel that she could not do what she had done again and that she needed to change her outlook. Raquel turned to me and said, 'Shut up! You would not know what its f---ing like. Imagine being raped. That is what happened to me over a period of time. Do you know what that is like? I am a victim of rape!' It was her tactic for putting me back in my place and it almost worked again. By the time the last words came out of her mouth she was right up in my face, staring me straight in the eyes. I could feel anger, hatred and guilt that she had harnessed for so many years exude from every pore of her body.

When someone says such things to you it is easy not to respond but to back off. However I decided that enough was enough and that I would return service as quickly and as sharply as I could. I said in a very stern voice: 'You know what, Raquel? You are right. I do not know what it is like to be in your situation. I could not ever know the amount of pain you must be feeling or how much you must be suffering.' My face tightened up as my glare into her eyes became even fiercer than it was. She slightly adjusted her body to a side stance and that was just the sign I needed to continue. I grabbed her shoulders and straightened her body to face me once again. I then said, 'You have been through so much. And I have so much sympathy for you, but you are *not* a victim. You are not a victim of rape.' I repeated and increased the volume a couple more notches. 'You *were* a victim Raquel. That is what you *were*. You are *now* a survivor.'

I then stood by her side and marked an invisible line on the wooden floorboards with my feet. 'This is where you *were*, Raquel. This is when you were a victim.' I then grabbed her hand with mine and clasped it tightly then took three steps forward, dragging her along with me. 'This is where you are now. That was your past Raquel; you are a survivor!' She remained silent while the strong facade she maintained earlier left her face, as though it was swept away by a sudden gust of wind. She was taking in everything that I had to say and it appeared as though she was in complete acceptance of a new perspective on what had happened, and with a new outlook on life.

For Raquel, this day marked the beginning of a trans-formation. With help, she learnt how to accept the fact she that couldn't change her past, and that the only way to peace and freedom was by moving forward. Today, Raquel is a woman tremendously far from self-harm and low self-worth. She has transformed her pain and suffering into motivation and passion and uses her experiences to assist the multitude of women affected by violence. This was evident in a conversation that I had with her some months after. She said to me candidly, 'I would never wish for anyone to be in my situation, but the fact is it happens to so many in our society. It has caused me so much pain, but now I am able to see that I am in a position to use my experiences to help the millions and millions of women around the world who do not have the strength or the support I have received. I feel blessed.'

Where Raquel had once seen a road of suffering, she now saw an opportunity to use her unfortunate situation to help others in a similar position. I was so proud of her; she had made it through.

The above story is a very extreme case which illustrates the power of our thoughts, both Conscious and subconscious, and how they can be so damaging. But, the way we perceive events and people impacts on us all every day. For instance, there was a time in my life when I didn't consider myself a 'morning person'. I detested hearing my alarm in the morning and just wanted to stay in bed. I would roll out of bed in a zombie-like state, turn on the television automatically to have background sound, take a quick shower, get changed, then buy the most popular newspaper to read with my breakfast, before I left to go to my football club for a day of work. This was my daily routine for quite some time. However as I became more aware of the importance of utilising the Conscious mind, I began to audit my life. Through this process, I realised that I was relinquishing an important opportunity to gain control of my Conscious mind, which would in turn make it easier for me to create the world I wanted to live in. I identified that I was giving up the first opportunity to start my day off on a positive note to the external powers of media. By automatically turning on the television, then going out and buying the paper, I was at the mercy of external influences.

In his book *The Greatness Guide*, Robin Sharma speaks about what he calls your 'holy hour'. The holy hour is the first hour of your day, and Robin Sharma says that one of the secrets of having a fulfilled day is focusing on the holy hour and being productive in it. I began to adopt this theory and change my behaviour in the morning by utilising my 'holy hour'.

I began to become more observant in the mornings by understanding how important the start to the day was in my life. I also started to see how much the media had influenced my world view. I wished that I had learnt about the importance of gaining a working understanding of how our minds work. I noticed that the vast majority of news reported by the media was negative and that it sensationalised what was actually occurring. I knew this to be true, because I had witnessed the way the media operated in my industry as a professional footballer, fabricating stories of high drama from rumours or speculation in an attempt to entertain. I decided to set aside more time for my own personal development, such as taking time to read books about inspirational lives and stories, to ensure that I was more in control of what went into my mind.

During the time when I began to become more conscious of what I was consuming intellectually, a great mentor of mine, Sakiya Sandifer, told me that the human mind is just like a big sponge: when you apply pressure to it, just like a sponge, what is inside comes out. This was when I really began to notice that I was taking back control of my mind.

Becoming Conscious in life means that you wake up from the surface where you are suspended, knowing that there is a lot more to the story than meets the eye. Observe your own life and see how your own mind works. Observe whether or not your fears and limitations are paralleled by the limitations and fears that are constantly fed to you on a daily basis through all forms of media. Just like me, you will find that your limitations and fears are heavily developed by thoughts that are not your own, rather they are those of people who do not have the power to create your life. So why allow these thoughts and emotions that are not yours to control and create your world?

Now we must also understand that a thought is energy. Experts in fields such as neuroscience and endocrinology tell us that a thought evokes a chemical response, which is energy. Energy is a vibration. When you have a thought about something negative, the consequent negative hormone will kick in. So understanding what we take in is crucial.

Think about how the mainstream media works. The mainstream media is not an entity unto itself. I hear a lot of people complain that the papers just print rubbish. A lot of those people actually have things printed about *them* and they complain, 'This paper is so bad!' People in society know what is negative; they know that mainstream media is having a negative effect, or they know that it is not serving them any purpose. Yet they still continue to pay for it.

Everything is interrelated and is fuelled by demand. Supply is fuelled by demand. Mainstream media, in actual fact, reflects and shapes society; in many ways it reflects a collective in society to some degree. Through observation, you realise that the mainstream media, such as the tabloids or even the evening news, works not to inform but to entertain. The more you can entertain people, the more people you will get observing. If it was just information presented in a particular way, then it would lose its popularity.

The fact is, the collective in our society is addicted to drama. You might say that this is a bold statement. But when you observe, you will see this to be quite accurate. Demand for tabloid media is shooting through the roof. We see how the paparazzi influence people with public profiles. We see how the tabloid media operates. We see how reality TV is becoming increasingly popular, due to the drama that it presents. So the drama that our collective society thrives on (our news, so to speak), is presented to us in a way that evokes those emotional responses we are addicted to and that entertain us. This is the reason that, while people complain about how terrible the news is, they still continue to watch it, knowing that it has no real substance. They know that they can get it from other sources which are a lot more informative, but presented in a different way. But people desire to be entertained, and the news is a form of entertainment because it is real life, and they can relate to it.

By observing what you consume, how it affects your life and the way that you look at the world, you will better understand the effects that this has on you. You will gain a better understanding about whether you're living in the grandstand or in the arena. The fact is, if what you're consuming is the news that entertains, then that is what's keeping you from the arena. The way that you look at things will, in fact, be what they are presenting. What you consume by way of mass media influences not only your Conscious mind, remember, but also your Conscious decision to actually take in these forms of news or this information. It will be subconscious, in that part of the mind you do not have direct control over. And this will spill out into other areas of your life. You will see that you not only seek drama in the form of the entertainment that you consume, but your life will be filled with drama; with ups and downs, whether in relationships, your workplace, or other areas of your life.

So, how you start your day is absolutely crucial to becoming Conscious. Are you starting your day with a Conscious decision to consume negative thoughts? Try beginning your day with positivity. It's a great way to start moving towards the arena.

I like to call the mainstream media and the way that it operates a circus. It has all the attractions: a trapeze artist, a lion tamer and a knife swallower—all the things that are attractive when creating a circus. However this form of entertainment, or this circus, is not proactive if you allow it to control your life. Lots of people allow it to control their lives. Many people's world views, values or perceptions of life are actually controlled by our mainstream media. A great way to observe what you take in is to recognise your desire for drama, and that can spill over into gossip.

In reality, the media is a huge part of how the world communicates. So I'm not telling you to eradicate it from your life completely. I'm simply suggesting that you make a Conscious effort to see it for what it is, without letting it influence how you want to see the world. The sooner you can move beyond this, the sooner you will be free to actually think the way *you* want to think.

On a basic level, we know our mind is divided into the Conscious mind and the subconscious mind, similar to the team and the coach. The team appears to be what's active out on the playing field, but the coach is the driving force behind the players. Our thoughts shape the way we look at the world and my understanding is that these are subconscious thoughts—ideas and behaviours that we've learnt over time that we don't really think about. They come to the surface on their own, and a lot of the time we unconsciously take them in as the truth.

Thoughts move from the depths of our subconscious up into the Conscious level, and that's when we can actually control them. If we want to **become Conscious**, our job is to influence the thoughts that shape our world with our Conscious mind. So, how do we do that?

BE CONSCIOUS OF LABELS

The first way to gain control of your mind is to notice how heavily it relies on labels. Once you recognise that your mind puts everything into boxes, you hear yourself saying things like: 'this is good', 'this is annoying', 'that person is angry', 'that person is cool' and so on. When you understand that labels are just a category created by your mind, you can start changing your thoughts and let the labels disappear.

The reason you want to get rid of the mind's labels is because they set limitations and prevent you from growing. What I mean by 'labels' are the definitions that we have for things, like 'good' or 'bad'. We constantly define things, whether they're objects or ideas. I'm not saying we should go through life pretending that nothing has a label, because the reason we name and label is to understand what's going on around us. Without labels, we wouldn't be able to communicate. We wouldn't know one football team from another. For us to be fully engaged in this world, we need to reference things with names. However, it can cause a lot of problems, because the name is just a name; it's just a reference point. Once you label something, you limit it. And once you limit something, you disregard its infinite nature and you miss out on the possibility to realise something you didn't know before. This factor may cause you to live life from a semi-conscious mindset.

Defining things is important, because we need it to gain understanding. When you begin to discover the magic of the arena, you become undefined. You still have values and ideals, but they become more flexible. Lady Gaga once said that she doesn't want to be defined and Kanye West said that people try to put labels on him but they don't stick. That's because they both understand that, when you define something, you limit it. And those guys didn't get where they are today by accepting the definitions other people may have given them.

Learn as much about yourself and the world as possible, in order to become Conscious. Then dismiss some of the labels people have given you, including the ones you give yourself.

It's common for us to give labels that relate to our morality: what's good and what's bad, what's right and what's wrong? Is this **good** or is this **bad**? Is this **right** or is this **wrong**? We automatically stick labels on everything we come across. But these notions don't really exist; they're man-made and they're constantly changing.

Take the notions of 'good' and 'bad' as an example. Roughly 50 years ago in the United States, lynching was accepted by a significant number of people. Look back another 200 years into history, and people thought it was right to burn women at the stake because they were supposedly witches. Today we have universally decided that lynching people for their skin colour or burning people for practising herbal medicine is wrong, but in the past it was public entertainment. It took people some time to open up their minds and take a different view of what is 'good' or 'bad' to see the real picture. Somehow, our thinking had to change so we could get to a new truth and make new decisions based on that.

> Between the notion of wrong doing and right doing there is a field—you will find me there.
>
> Rumi, Sufi mystic and poet

Racism is just one example of the detrimental effects of labelling. It's undesired, unfair and unjust and it all comes from labelling. It's crazy to call someone a name or to have prejudice against them just because of their ethnicity. A person's skin colour or religion does not define them; there is so much more to all of us than that.

One of the reasons racism still exists in our world today because of labelling. I've experienced racism all my life, but I realised early on that it was just down to people not seeing our similarities because they were focusing on the fact that I'm black. But the truth is, underneath our skin, we're actually all the same. We put labels on each other, like tall, short, black or whatever, as a way of defining and understanding. It's ironic that our need for using labels to understand each other can also be a cause of racism.

A study by Paul Ekman shows that expressions among all nationalities are universal. We all show the same facial expressions for the same emotions or use words relating to a particular emotion in our respective languages, which I think is pretty cool. It just goes to show that, while we may have different appearances, speak in different languages and live in different locations, we all feel the same emotions and we can see this through our expressions.

We're able to understand that this is all just superficial stuff. There is a deeper truth and, once we find it, it lifts us up and dissolves any conflicts we have with the world. Using racism as an example, it often occurs because of previous experiences. Let's say a Latino man shoots a shopkeeper in America. The shop owner survives but, because of that one incident, he now considers all Latino people to be savage and terrible. Every time he serves a Latino person in his shop, his heart shudders because this new person has a particular thing in common with his perpetrator. And that common thing is the label. He thinks 'Latinos are bad' but it's not true; not everyone from a single race is bad, just because a few behave in a certain way. We all label things 'good' or 'bad', 'right' or 'wrong'. But when we use the labels to put people into boxes, instead of as a means to understand or communicate, we cause problems for ourselves and humanity, because the label becomes the only thing we see.

It's like His Holiness the Dalai Lama says:

When you think that your neighbours have nothing to do with your own happiness, you mistreat them.

Because of my experiences, I've managed not to put people in boxes. I was labelled because I was seen as being different, rather than the same as the kids in my neighbourhood. I had to create more 'sameness', which is where playing footy came in.

The first time I can recall coming to terms with the negative effect of labelling was when I was nine years old, playing football in the Under 10s in Perth. The team I was playing for at the time was having a great season and were on top of the ladder and set to play against the number two team in our next game. For that whole week, I remember thinking about that important game nonstop. It was the first time that the result of a football game meant so much to me. As a nine-year-old footballer, I showed a lot of natural ability and was regarded as one of the league's best players for my age.

Trying to understand and accept my identity at that young age was challenging, and at times confusing, due to my unique cultural identity. I just wanted to feel normal and connected to something greater than myself. Sport, and football in particular, was one area where I could feel normal and equal. Parents would compliment me on how valued I was to my team and my teammates would tell me that they were so glad that I was on their team. This was crucial to my self-esteem.

However one day the football field, my safe haven, became a place of great torment and I still carry strong memories of the experience to this day. In Under 10 competitive football, the 'competitive' aspect of the game is certainly there; young kids well and truly understand the difference between winning and losing and the emphasis society places on both. Before this particular game, I remember feeling that there was even more emphasis than usual placed on the result, by the families and players of both teams. These were the games that I loved, and I can recall my older brother Gabriel telling me prior to the game: 'These are the kind of games where you find out who the star players are; the big games!' He was trying to wind me up and perhaps motivate me, but I can vividly remember that I did not need anyone to motivate me at that time. I was so determined to play the best game of my life.

Just as the game commenced, I noticed something was occurring that had never happened to me before. I turned to both my left and right and noticed that there were two players playing on me. From the word go, they began to harass me physically, by bumping into me and pushing me. I laughed and said, 'The two of you will never be able to keep up with me today.' They seemed to make eye contact with one another, then pushed and bumped me once more. It was obvious that they were under clear instructions from their coach to try and put me off my game. 'That's it boys, get under his skin!' the coach yelled enthusiastically to the two boys.

About five minutes into the game, I still had my two shadows and they did not look like leaving my side. In fact, they did not even look like touching the ball, because they didn't once have their eyes on it; their sole focus was me. This is when they began to play against the rules. Every time I tried to go near the ball, one of the boys would grab me. This type of treatment was foreign to me and I began to retaliate by pushing back. The next few times I swore at them and told them to go for the ball. They chuckled and said, 'What's the matter? Are we putting you off your game?' I ignored them. Towards the end of the quarter, I had hardly seen any of the play; I was kept unusually quiet and my frustration was growing at the opposition's lack of sportsmanship.

Then the ball spilled free near me. This time I tried even harder to get the ball in my possession, to try to make up for my lack of influence on the game. It worked; I managed to break free and cleanly pick up the loose ball from the ground, run ten metres, and then deliver the ball forward towards goal. It was a great bit of play for a nine-year-old and, judging by the spectators' reactions, they were impressed.

Moments after the ball had left my area, I was bumped in the back then shoved in the side by my two new acquaintances. One of them said to me, 'You got lucky there, you coon.' I tried to ignore this because I really did not know what to do, nor did I want them to know that what they'd just said really did cut deep into me.

The other boy began to chime in, 'What's wrong? Are we making you play bad?' He had a smug little smirk on his face and that's when I retorted with aggression, 'You guys are only doing this because I am better than you and you cannot beat me if you play fair.' The boy who called me a coon must have sensed that discrimination would work best against me and said, 'At least we're not black like you, you coon.' Once again, I did not know what to do because, up until that point in my life, no-one had ever been so blatant with racial discrimination directed at me. My head began to spin, and it seemed like everything except those two boys had dissolved around me. I was no longer on a football field but inside what seemed to be a terrible nightmare. Tears started to roll down my cheeks, as both boys started to jeer me by repeatedly saying the word 'boong' (a derogatory term which has similar weight in Australia to the words *nigger* and *kaffir*).

My head began to feel like it was going to explode, and that's when I began to run in the opposite direction to where the ball was. Everyone noticed that I was now running off the field like a maniac and began to call out my name, but I just kept running. When I heard my stepfather's voice, I stopped in my tracks and looked over my shoulder and saw that he was running after me. When he got up to me, he put his arm on my shoulder and I began to cry. Somehow he already knew what had happened. I told him that I would never play football again. He didn't say anything; he just walked with me to our car, with his arm on my shoulder. When we got in the car, he told me that it had only occurred because the boys were the ones with an issue, and that I was certainly not to blame for the unfair behaviour. He told me it would be tough, but that this would be a great learning experience for me.

The next day my stepfather told me he was going to take me to do the weekly grocery shopping but instead had organised for me to meet one of my childhood heroes, who had recently retired from the AFL. His name was Derek Kickett; he was an indigenous player that I admired dearly and had been my favourite player at the football club I once supported. My stepfather had organised to take me to a WAFL game in which he was playing (WAFL is one level below AFL in Western Australia). I watched the game with great joy, as Derek kicked four goals.

After the game, we were met by a man who my Dad seemed to know. As I followed my stepfather and this man, I was trying to figure out where exactly they were going; that's when we began to make our way into the Subiaco change rooms. I was in awe! It was the first time in my life I had ever been inside 'real' football change rooms. The man then disappeared for a moment and I stood at the doorway with my stepfather. When he returned, he was with my old hero, Derek Kickett. Derek introduced himself to us, and then told me to come with him. He put his arm around my shoulder and walked me around the change rooms. We found a quiet place in the corner of the rooms and sat down. He asked me what had happened, and listened intently while shaking his head in disappointment. He then told me that he had experienced the same thing many times before. He emphasised that it was not my fault and said that people who resort to racism only do so because they are insecure, incompetent and afraid of their victims. I remember feeling at the time that it was amazing to know someone who understood exactly what I was going through at the time.

After we hung out for a while, my stepfather came back over and thanked Derek for everything. I left the change rooms with the biggest smile on my face, which stayed there for the entire week. It gave me enough inspiration to come out of my early retirement and play again!

This was the first time I experienced blatant racism and it certainly was not the last. However, every time I experienced racial discrimination, I was able to draw on that experience and not let it emotionally destroy me, like the first time. The more I witnessed and experienced racial discrimination, the more interested I became in understanding why it exists. This interest set me off on a journey to study the likes of Nelson Mandela, Martin Luther King Jr and Malcolm X. Just like me, these men all had to overcome prejudice. Their personal stories and wisdom helped shape my understanding of why such things occur. Most importantly, their testimonies taught me not to be afraid to stand up and show people the way through leadership, self-belief and passion.

Labels just keep us in our comfort zone but the result is that we'll never experience life inside the arena. When you choose not to define things, like the people around you, that's when you'll see the full story.

You might be asking, 'Why should I stop labelling things? Isn't winning 'good' and losing 'bad'? Well sure, it feels good when you win and not so good when you lose, but they're really just words to describe feelings. If we can set aside the need to label everything and just accept a situation for what it is—a game of football for example— then that's the breakthrough. And it doesn't reduce your desire to do your best. What it does is release your attachment to the outcome, which means you'll still give it your all, just without the need for labelling. I've found that, since I dropped the need to label my experiences as 'good' or 'bad', I've become able to stay more centred in both my footy game and my regular life.

It works in our favour to stop relying on labelling to tell us the full story. When we go beyond this, we discover we can use the arena to assist us in any way we choose. If you're always watching from the grandstand you won't see the full story; and when you are stuck in the world of labelling and defining, you will miss out on the infinite possibilities the world has to offer. It might be the people that you meet—and there are so many examples of those who miss their opportunity or their break, because they chose not to speak to someone. Could that person on the tram on the way to the game be the key to you unlocking your dreams? Could that person assist you in life? Did you choose not to speak to that person because of his or her appearance? So remember, next time you think there might be the chance of an opportunity, go for it!

CONSCIOUS TIPS TO REMEMBER

- You don't have to fully understand how your mind works, in order to reap the benefits and get the best out of its capabilities.

- Take the time to carefully observe your thoughts. Your thoughts shape your reality. Change the way you see the world, by thinking positively.

- Observe what you take in on a Conscious level, and be aware how this affects your subconscious thoughts.

- Avoid getting caught up in the drama created by the media. Be Conscious of what you take in and choose to start your day by taking in positive information.

- Your mind's labels limit you and prevent you from growing. Consciously remove labels one by one, and then start seeing possibilities that have been previously overlooked.

- Remove labels to see the full story. Opinions of others will always exist but don't let them influence how you see the world. You have the ability to make your own decisions.

- We need some labels in order to communicate, but don't let labels limit or cloud your thoughts. Labels are man-made and constantly change.

- Negative images and information evoke negative emotions. Be mindful of what you see, hear and read. Don't let outside negativity influence how you view the world.

- Know that labels are just categories created by your mind to organise information. When you change your thinking, the labels will disappear and the true nature and beauty of everything will shine through.
- Use labels as a reference point only!

FOREWORD by Deepak Chopra:

There are many types of meditation. There's visualisation, sound, smell and affirmations. These are all useful forms of meditation and can bring about healing. But they are all based on mental activity. I use a type of meditation that takes you beyond the mind, to the individual soul, and finally to the spirit, or universal Consciousness. This is called Primordial Sound Meditation.

Sound is the first code of intelligence, the first movement of Consciousness. Thinking is also a form of hearing. We hear our thoughts, and since thinking is the subtlest form of activity, sound is the subtlest of all our experiences. The essence of sound is the primordial sound. Mantras are primordial sounds, the essence of which is pure Consciousness. Over the years, I have found that using mantras (Primordial Sound Meditation) is the best form of meditation for me.

Never judge the quality of your meditation. Once you get results, you'll know you are doing it correctly. When you become aware of the fact you are thinking, you shift your attention back to the mantra. As you continue to do this, your thoughts become fainter and fainter. Suddenly the thoughts disappear. What remains is the one who witnesses and creates these thoughts. You are now in touch with your soul, with your own essential state.

PILLAR 4:
STILL THE MIND THROUGH MEDITATION

> *To the mind that is still,*
> *the whole universe surrenders.*
>
> Lao Tzu, Chinese philosopher, founder of Taoism

The **fourth pillar** is meditation. Before you sigh 'Oh no' and ask, 'Great, do I have to go to Tibet, sit on the side of a mountain and contemplate my navel to put it into practice?' the answer is definitely 'no'. Meditation is a powerful tool that each and every one of us can practise whenever we choose. Through meditation, we're able to tap into our own Consciousness at any time and, from some of the earlier stories in this book, you'll have seen how it has helped me deal with some really difficult times in my life. This chapter will further draw your attention to the value of meditation and show how daily (or regular) practice can help you on your way to living a full and Conscious life.

Sometimes, people don't discover the magic of living in the arena because the grass may be slightly muddy, and they don't want to get their feet stuck or dirty. But once you discover what it opens you up to and see that mud just dries and washes off, you realise the possibilities that were always there. You then come to the understanding of 'Gee, why didn't I play earlier?' And that's okay, because you can continue to go there and stay on the field; the choice is yours.

Some people are able to see the perfectly-cut green grass with all the right markings that haven't faded, so it's easy for them to make the transition from the grandstand. The notion I'd like to raise is that we are **all** able to take control of how our lives look, and so create calmness and order in everything we do. The best way to do this is through one of the many forms of meditation.

THE VALUE OF MEDITATION

On the topic of meditation and contemplation, Deepak Chopra has written:

> As more and more people meditate, the collective Consciousness of humanity will evolve with greater connection to spirit and greater conceptuality of principles which foster compassion, nurturing and abundance.

By understanding this, or even having knowledge of this, we start to realise that meditation raises Consciousness.

Meditation is something that I use regularly to assist me in my busy daily life.

In Western society, the notion of meditation can be a bit extreme. We often think of meditation as a religion or something spiritual. It's common to be told you're 'off with the fairies' or a 'hippie' or some other untrue connotation. I've seen this notion stop people from accessing this arena. But we can all use this powerful tool to help us create the life that we want. Deepak Chopra has said:

> *The purpose of meditation is to take us into the field of infinite possibilities, to go into the gap between the thoughts, then to come back here in order to create according to our dreams.*

What I take from his words is that, when we give ourselves the opportunity to be still, cut out the chatter in our mind and turn inwards, then what we really desire and strive towards starts to become clear. We become open to opportunities and see everything in our lives holistically, which ultimately leads us to a world of infinite possibilities.

Primordial sound meditation is recommended by Deepak Chopra, to help us all get to that special place when thoughts disappear, as mentioned in his Foreword to this chapter. The word 'mantra' means 'instrument of thought' in the ancient language of Sanskrit. Repeating a mantra might be a useful way to help you meditate, especially if you feel you just can't calm your mind. While there are various mantras for different outcomes, I'd suggest that you repeat the mantra 'Om' or 'Aum'. This is the sound of the universe and also signifies becoming one with all.

You may not be aware of this, but meditation creates a biological reaction that leads to positive benefits such as a greater wellbeing. There are many studies conducted by educational institutions on the benefits of meditation and its effect on our physiology. Without adding a ton of scientific jargon—which could distract or confuse you—meditation is basically an effective tool for reducing stress.

Daily meditation helps to regulate the cortisol levels in our body. Cortisol is released as a stress response to bring our bodies back to their natural balanced state. Meditation is another way to become more balanced and Conscious, because it helps us to see clearly. So instead of seeing a muddy playing surface, we see a vibrant arena that we'll feel comfortable running onto. If the arena remains bright and inviting, we'll be able to start kicking winning goals straight away.

Connecting with our Conscious self through meditation gives us the ability to see so much more than the everyday stuff that's going on. It's a way of clearing the mind from unwanted distractions that we get tangled up with over time.

In recent years, I've noticed how easy it is to lose control of your thoughts and affect your perspective on life. As an example, I've noticed that, when I am tired, my thoughts can become quite negative. I become impatient and agitated and, as a result, I am more likely to have bad experiences.

We can all lose control of our perspective when confronted with pressure and stress. Every tragedy or failure presents a great opportunity to learn the most valuable lessons in life and develop one of its most valuable qualities—resilience.

What separates a rookie from a veteran? The first year rookie usually lacks confidence because he fears making mistakes, so he performs tentatively which affects his overall effectiveness. The ten year veteran is all too familiar with what to expect. He is not overawed by the experience because he has done it all before and no longer feels under pressure. He is aware and concedes that he will make mistakes; however he knows that it is part of the game and does not fear making them. And when he does make a mistake, he is not caught lamenting over it for too long: he gets on with the game and doesn't let negative thoughts affect his confidence. The rookie can allow one minor mistake to affect his entire mindset, compromising performance.

One of the hardest things to develop is resilience. Resilience is a capacity developed through struggle. Unfortunately, not everyone who struggles in life gains resilience; in fact, many people actually become less resilient as a result of struggle. Resilience is the ability to have control over how you withstand the tough times of pressure and stress.

Resilience is built up by taking control of your mind. After you make a mistake or something 'bad' happens, it is human nature to allow it to affect you in a negative way. It is very easy to drop your head and start to see everything from that point on as 'bad'. If you are playing sport and you miss a shot or a goal, resilience is the quality that allows you to get on with the job and make sure that, when you get your next opportunity, your performance is not affected by your failure. But how do you develop that?

The answer is to start off simply at the level of thought. Resilience is ignoring all the 'bad' thoughts that arise by choosing to generate and listen to the 'good' thoughts. This ability to create and choose to listen only to good thoughts is a skill that is developed over time. However, this process can be fast-tracked by using meditation. When you get into a routine of regular mediation, you gain the ability to become detached from your thoughts and to simply watch them pass through your awareness. The ability to do this becomes extremely valuable in times of stress and pressure, because it prevents you from becoming overwhelmed by fear.

In Collingwood's 2010 Grand Final victory, my practice of meditation played an integral part in my kicking a memorable goal, which I'll cherish of the rest of my life. Early on in that game, I had the opportunity to kick the first goal of the Grand Final replay. It was a set shot from long range and with a bit of an angle. I remember going through the routine that I'd developed over the years—the most effective goal kicking routine for me. Unfortunately I did not execute the desired result. In fact, the kick was horrible and missed by a considerable amount. After the kick, I immediately lamented the missed opportunity and thought to myself that I rarely had opportunities to kick goals, as I was playing in defence at the time. In the last quarter, I had a chance to redeem myself, with a chance to kick at goal from exactly the same distance and angle as before. This time a goal would mean a lot more to the team, as it would almost certainly cement our victory.

I remember that, before going into my routine, the ramifications of either scoring or missing the shot were dominant thoughts in my head. Then I decided to control my breathing, just as I do in my meditations and to try and 'detach' from all thoughts, other than following my goal kicking routine. I was able to let negative thoughts pass through my mind, until they began to diminish and then disappear altogether. I felt as though nothing existed but me and my goal kicking routine. I couldn't even hear the crowd at this point. I was able to do my routine the way I had practised it many times before on the training track, where there was less pressure and thus easier to concentrate and kick effectively.

This ability to withdraw and detach from negative thoughts derived from fear allowed me not to let my previous miss in the first quarter affect my performance, it allowed me to score a famous Grand Final goal. Meditation no doubt helped me develop the ability to clear and control my mind when I needed to.

An untrained mind is an out-of-control mind. And when your mind is out of control, your life may feel out of control. The great thing about the mind is that it's like a muscle, which can be trained in the same the way that a body builder increases their chest or biceps. Body builders do weight training and resistance stretching to influence the capacity of their muscles. Meditation does the same thing, only it influences the capacity of the mind— one of the most incredible tools we have.

Meditation allows you to see that you are *not* your mind, and that thoughts have a transient nature that's ever-changing. That's why it's good to keep your thoughts in check. Dr Wayne Dyer, writes a lot about this in his books. In *The Power of Intention*, he breaks it down and makes things easy with the following example:

Instead of saying to yourself 'I hate this place we're living in, it gives me the creeps', you can turn it into a positive, such as 'I can see our new home in my mind, and I intend to be living in it within six months.'

PRACTISING MINDFULNESS

Keeping thoughts in check can be difficult in the beginning, because we're not used to pondering every thought we have; they just seem to come to us naturally. A great way to be Conscious of your thoughts is to practise mindfulness, which is often used by Buddhists. Being mindful is to simply spend some time with your own mind, with your own thoughts, actions and movements at that particular moment. It helps you stay in the present and raises your awareness of what's going on around you, as well as in your mind.

Being mindful can also mean your experiences are much more fulfilling. For example, most of us have a weekly routine and walking to the bus stop might be part of it. We may leave the house, lock the door, walk two blocks to the bus stop and on arrival we don't remember anything along the way. The one thing we do know is that we're not in the mood for a 9am start at the office. We have the ability to make this little daily trip a lot more fulfilling by being mindful. Think of each step you take, notice the houses, are there other people walking on the street? Perhaps you could say 'hello' to them. You could start being mindful of what you're thinking about on your walk—is it about work or perhaps the person you are meeting during your lunch break? The point is, it's about giving your full attention to something and being aware of what's around you, without reacting or having strong feelings about it.

The more you practise mindfulness, the more Conscious you'll become. It's such a simple tool, yet so effective for becoming Conscious. In fact, mindfulness is the first step that Buddhists take before meditation. So, if the thought of meditating for the first time seems impossible, due to the millions of thoughts rushing around your mind, you might like to sit for a moment and start being mindful of what you're actually thinking about. Then choose to let your thoughts slowly drift away. The great thing is, once you've done this, you'll be able to tune in and experience the clarity that meditation brings.

Let me share with you a time when I felt my life was out of control but I managed to rise above that difficult situation by practising mindfulness.

2012 was an extremely difficult year for me for various reasons. I felt the accumulated weight of the tragedies and traumas I had experienced in recent years come crashing down on me. The year started off badly for me, as I was suffering from post traumatic stress, due to an incident that I had witnessed in Rio de Janeiro on Christmas Day 2011. That experience really affected me and caused me to have a negative lens throughout most of the year. I was still able to will myself to see things positively, however I had failed to really deal with my past. Looking back, it is now evident that my past haunted me on numerous occasions. Despite lacking intrinsic motivation, I found just enough energy to get by with football, but my performances were certainly below par for my standards and expectations.

Just when I thought things could not get any worse and my faith in life could not fall any lower, a terrible tragedy struck our football club. On Monday 10 September, we arrived at the Westpac Centre for a normal training session. Before training had even begun, we were called into a meeting by our CEO Gary Pert—a very unusual occurrence. In that meeting, Gary informed us that our ex-teammate John McCarthy had tragically fallen to his death from the top of a hotel, while on his end of season football trip to Las Vegas.

I remember instantly feeling my head start to spin as heard my teammates' cries of pain. I put my head in my hands and began to cry (uncontrollably). I remembered John's extremely kind and polite nature; he was a great young man. Then thoughts started to fire through my mind at a million miles an hour. My mind took me back to the scenes I had witnessed in Rio de Janeiro and the smell of my stepfather's decomposing body. I was conscious of the immense pain the McCarthy family were no doubt feeling. It was a pain that I remembered and was feeling once again.

Death is as much a part of life as life itself; but to lose life at such a young age and in such tragic circumstances makes one ask many questions about the justice of life.

Life can be so cruel and, at that particular moment in my life, I had lost full faith in everything.

I remember after that meeting all the players slowly made their way back into the locker rooms and cried in each other's arms to console one another. It was great to know that you were not alone. But everyone deals with tragedy in different ways and I know that I did not cope well at all with John's death. For a period of time following that tragedy I sunk to some of the darkest times I had ever faced. It was only through a conscious and calculated way that I was able to climb my way out of what seemed to be a very dark hole.

The first thing I did was realise that I was in an extremely bad place. I knew that, if I did not do something about making a positive change, I would continue feeling as terrible as I was, which was very destructive. I identified that I had not fully resolved my past and could not possibly move forward if I didn't attempt to work through the many issues that I had put to the back of my mind.

I decided that I could not and should not have to do it alone, and I sought professional help. My therapist helped me identify the unresolved issues that I had put to the back of my mind and then we began to work on them. This was the beginning of a positive change in my mind; I felt as though I was making progress on issues I had neglected to confront in my past.

I was given specific targets to aim for including becoming as healthy as possible and putting my wellbeing as the number one priority in life. I changed everything, from the food I was eating to the amount of sleep I was getting to ensure I was investing everything into my wellbeing.

My recent experiences with death had taught me how fickle life can really be, so I decided that I wanted to try to make the most out of my life. I decided to try a bit of an experiment which resulted in a complete change to my perspective on life. Throughout my life, I had heard the cliché *Live everyday as though it is your last* bandied around by many people. It is a subtle reminder to make the most of your life by living in the present moment. One morning when I woke up that cliché was on my mind. I couldn't get it out of my head so I decided I would try to literally live that day as if it were my last.

The rule I made for this experiment was that I had to follow my normal daily routine. Obviously, if it were my last day on earth, I would definitely try to be as close to my loved ones as possible. The first thing I did that morning was go through my phone and send a personalised text message to all of my loved ones. After sending individual personalised messages to over 70 contacts in my phone I noticed that I felt extremely good—I had taken the time to appreciate and reflect on how important those people had been in my life. After sending those text messages, it was time for breakfast. Keeping with my usual routine I had a bowl of muesli with some fruit. I reminded myself that it was the 'last' time I would be having breakfast, so I really paid attention to the taste of the food I was eating. It seemed to taste a lot nicer than on previous days, because I was not rushing to get it down nor was I preoccupied with anything else, like browsing the internet.

As I left home for football training, I made a playlist of my favourite songs because, if it were my last day on this planet, I would want to listen to my favourite music. This immediately got me feeling happy so as I was driving into my football club I was already in a good mood. In fact, while I was sitting in morning traffic, I paid extra attention to little things that I had not even considered before. Street art seemed to be extra special to me; an old couple walking by on the footpath brought a smile to my face; and I took the time to be appreciative of the fact that I had a car to drive.

By the time I arrived at the football club, I had already received over 20 text messages of appreciation from loved ones, in reply to my earlier messages. Each reply brought a smile to my face. I remember feeling that I had started the day off in amazing fashion. I reminded myself that it was the 'last' time I would be at the football club, so I decided to try to have as positive an impact on the training day as possible. That day on the training track I seemed to have more energy than previously and I enjoyed and savoured every single moment of training. Even my coaches noticed and I was told by a few people that they really could see my enthusiasm and intensity making a positive impact on the rest of the team. This just made me feel even better. Even though I made some mistakes at training they were quickly forgotten, as I didn't allow any error to impact on my next opportunities.

By the time I had spent the full working day at the football club, I had received a reply from most of the people I had sent a morning SMS to. I remember driving home that day from the club with the biggest smile on my face and feeling as though I had really got the most out of the day. I was satisfied that I had 'finished off' at the club on such a positive note.

After having dinner and getting ready to go to bed, I took the time to think about what a positive day I had had. I realised that my little experiment had simply forced me to live in the present moment and, by doing so, I began to see the beauty rather than the flaws in everything in life. This served as a great lesson for me, as it showed me that consciously living in the present moment will enhance life in an enormous way. I remember thinking to myself as I lay in my bed about to fall asleep that I had quite possibly experienced one of the best days of my life. And all I had done was shift my thoughts, so that I was in the present moment.

Just before I fell asleep, my favourite quote came to my mind and it was one of the last thoughts I had:

When you change the way you look at things, the things you look at change.

By creating my own thoughts and living in the moment, I managed to dig myself out of that low place and rise above it. That was the first time I'd really experienced the power of meditation and reflection, and I've personally never looked back.

When you meditate, it helps you realise your natural state of being. Your mind becomes less turbulent and more stable. Training your mind to think positively, in the way Wayne Dyer suggests, makes it much easier to believe that life can be good. Yes, you will still feel natural emotions like sadness and stress. However, when you become more Conscious, you move into a more balanced and clear state. You can then dive into the depths of life's incredible possibilities and find the infinite and unconditional treasure that awaits you every time.

Esther and Jerry Hicks talk about this all the time in their *Law of Attraction* series books. They say that we have the ability to direct our own thoughts and we can choose to observe things as they are, or imagine them as we want them to be. Both ways are equally powerful, because they create a vibration that can have amazing consequences. Esther and Jerry Hicks say that, to be the *Deliberate Creator* of your own experience, you have to decide to direct your thoughts. When you deliberately choose the direction of your own thoughts, you can deliberately affect your own point of attraction. Their view is that you cannot continue to believe things in the same way you always have, if you want to make a change.

Remember to be mindful or repeat a mantra, in order to empty your mind of unwanted thoughts and direct your mind to things or situations you'd like to see in your life. When I feel like I'm getting off track and the things around me aren't exactly how I'd like them to be, I reflect on the following quote by the Dalai Lama:

> *In order to change the external situation, we must first change within ourselves.*

It's amazing how a few words can make so much sense and help us to get on the path that we're meant to be on.

CONSCIOUS TIPS TO REMEMBER

- Meditation is something you can practise whenever you choose, in order to tap into your own Consciousness.
- Regular meditation will assist you in living a full and Conscious life.
- Meditation doesn't have to mean sitting on mountains in exotic locations; it has many forms. You may like to meditate in your room each morning, on waking up.
- Meditation is a great stress reducer. Regular practice will help you feel in control, as it helps train and clear the mind.
- Regular meditation is the key to unlocking the door to the life you'd like to live.
- Once you're a regular meditator, you'll soon see you can take it anywhere. Notice the great benefits that meditation has on your wellbeing.
- If you have an important event or meeting, then meditation is a great way to clear your mind and prepare yourself well.
- Meditation helps you understand that you're not your mind. Thoughts are transient! Meditation is an excellent way to monitor and direct your thoughts.

EPILOGUE

Now that you've begun to transcend the surface of life, you'll realise that this book isn't a step-by-step guide on how to live. You know now that I don't believe that there is a right or wrong or better or worse way to live. That's a completely subjective determination that some people make. I believe that life should be expressed in an infinite and unique way by every person.

It's Cool To Be Conscious shows us that we have a choice to transcend the surface of life: we have a choice to see what lies beyond the surface. The fact is, the vast majority of people tend to think or have the illusion that they are making that choice. But if they took a step back and looked objectively, they would realise that they have relinquished their divine right to create and understand what's real.

There are many ways in which you can dive beyond the surface. In this book, you've read about a few experiences in my life and some methods I have used to dive in and gain a deeper understanding about life.

Many people look at my life and see my experiences as being unique and unorthodox. In actual fact, these are just words which limit experiences. I believe that everyone's experiences are infinite and unique: nothing is ever created the same. Similar maybe, but never the same.

My experiences, which have given me the ability to gain this insight, have often involved initial suffering and pain. However, I have been able to transcend these experiences and gain a perspective on life which has brought about an understanding that many experiences are, in fact, unconscious. And when you wake up, you can see the true beauty that life has to offer. You see beauty in everything and you feel a connection to everything.

Once you realise that you are not separate from anything else, then you can see that anything can be yours. And once you see that anything can be yours, your desire for material things diminishes. This is what it means to be Conscious.

Hopefully you've realised that the four main chapters (the Pillars) in this book are more like four ideas or four ways in which you can begin to know yourself. I encourage you to use these ideas as a starting point to dive beyond the surface in your own life.

Imagine that you and I are snorkelling in crystal clear waters with beautiful sea life, or even treasure, below us. However, despite the fact that we have snorkelling gear and the ability to dive down, we are staying on top of the surface. So all we can see is the horizon, the crashing waves and the occasional ship or boat. Obviously that is not the full story. All we have to do is change our perception. If you shift the position of your head downwards and look below the surface of the water, you'll see the life—infinite life. And the deeper you go, the more you'll see. You'll see the infinite nature of all things. You'll see the life below you. You'll realise that you can go down and get the treasure and return to the surface with a new understanding and a new appreciation, because the act of diving below the surface actually defines the surface itself.

However, you'll never know what is below the surface if you do not dive. All you can know from being on the surface is what lies on the surface. This is not the true story; it is only a small fraction of it.

Keep striving to dive down below the surface; not just for a brief moment, but on a regular basis. Express the beauty that you find below the surface, perhaps through music, art, film, writing or sport? Do whatever works for you.

Our journey has begun. Let's continue to open our minds, strive to be our best and experience the sensation of being truly alive!

– Heritier

ABOUT HERITIER (HARRY) O'BRIEN

Harry O'Brien, born Heritier Deserbelles Lusevy Lumumba, is one of the Australian Football League's most recognisable players. He is currently the only Brazilian-born player in the AFL and, at just 27 years of age, he has certainly made a great impression in his playing career with the Collingwood Football Club over the last nine years.

Born in Rio de Janeiro to a Brazilian mother and a Congolese father, Harry moved to Melbourne in 1989 with his mother and older brother. In 1994, the family moved to Perth. Harry grew up in what would be considered an 'unorthodox' household—his family of six did not physically resemble him in the slightest. Harry was the only black member of the family, which includes three other siblings. He experienced racial discrimination from a young age and this significantly shaped his outlook on life and instilled in him a strong passion for human rights and social equality.

Aside from his outstanding on-field performances, Harry is also involved in many community projects and charities.

At age 16, he had his first experience of volunteer work, assisting with the Community Development Foundation, where he mentored indigenous primary school students. Since then, Harry has been involved with a number of charities and benevolent organisations, including the Salvation Army, The Burnet Institute, Hearts United For Humanity, and the Marley family's One Love Foundation. He has also been asked to speak at a number of events, including two United Nations conferences.

Harry is an AFL Multicultural Ambassador and People of Australia Ambassador. He was also an official ambassador for the Dalai Lama's visit to Australia in 2011. Meeting and talking to the Buddhist spiritual leader had a significant impact on Harry.

All of the things Harry is and has been involved with remain close to his heart. He is a strong believer in equal rights and continually campaigns for the support and recognition of those who feel displaced or disadvantaged.

PLAYING CAREER

In 2007, O'Brien enjoyed a meteoric rise to prominence as one of Collingwood Football Club's most important defenders. A success story of the 2004 rookie draft, he played four senior games in 2005, before earning permanent elevation to the senior list in 2006. Harry then enjoyed a superb 2007 season, in which he established himself as a regular senior player.

In 2008 Harry won the Jack Regan Trophy for finishing fifth in the Club's Best & Fairest after playing every game. In 2009 Harry also played every game (25), while averaging a career-high in disposals (16). He also won the JF McHale Trophy (fourth in Collingwood's Best & Fairest). In 2010, he played in Collingwood's all-conquering premiership side and also received the honour of being included in the All Australian Team for that season. And again in 2013, he won the Jack Regan Trophy in the Best and Fairest for fifth place. Today, Harry is still one of Collingwood's elite players

For further statistics and professional playing information, please go to http://www.collingwoodfc.com.au/player-profile/heritier-obrien

Connect with Harry:
Facebook:
www.facebook.com/harrysworld8

Twitter:
twitter.com/harry_o

ACKNOWLEDGEMENTS

There are many people who have made this book possible, in many ways.

Some realise it, and some don't.

Firstly, I'd like to thank all my coaches, teammates and administrators at my football club for accepting me for who I am and allowing me to express my ideas.

I would also like to thank my mother Elizabeth, sister Raquel and brothers Gabriel and Matthew for their unconditional love and support. I know great times are on the horizon for us all.

To my manager, Jess … you have been a guardian angel. Thank you for helping to keep it all together.

Of course, this book wouldn't have manifested itself if it wasn't for the team at Hay House. Leon, thank you so much for believing in my vision and trusting my ideas. Margie, Rosie and Hannah, thank you for your patience and guiding me through this process.

Finally, to all my mentors and teachers along the way who have shaped who I am today. Thank you: Deepak, Mike Toole, Philip Batterham, Fred Swann, Sakiya Sandifer, Traceye Smith.

We hope you enjoyed this Hay House book. If you'd like to receive our online catalogue featuring additional information on Hay House books and products, or if you'd like to find out more about the Hay Foundation, please contact:

Hay House Australia Pty. Ltd.,
18/36 Ralph St., Alexandria NSW 2015
Phone: +61 2 9669 4299 • *Fax:* +61 2 9669 4144
www.hayhouse.com.au

– – –

Published and distributed in the USA by: Hay House, Inc.,
P.O. Box 5100, Carlsbad, CA 92018-5100
Phone: (760) 431-7695 • *Fax:* (760) 431-6948
www.hayhouse.com® • www.hayfoundation.org

Published and distributed in the United Kingdom by:
Hay House UK, Ltd., Astley House, 33 Notting Hill Gate,
London, W11 3JQ • *Phone:* 44-203-675-2450
Fax: 44-203-675-2451 • www.hayhouse.co.uk

Published and distributed in the Republic of South Africa by:
Hay House SA (Pty), Ltd., P.O. Box 990, Witkoppen 2068
Phone/Fax: 27-11-467-8904 • www.hayhouse.co.za

Published in India by: Hay House Publishers India, Muskaan Complex,
Plot No. 3, B-2, Vasant Kunj, New Delhi 110 070
Phone: 91-11-4176-1620 • *Fax:* 91-11-4176-1630
www.hayhouse.co.in

Distributed in Canada by:
Raincoast, 9050 Shaughnessy St., Vancouver, B.C. V6P 6E5
Phone: (604) 323-7100 • *Fax:* (604) 323-2600 • www.raincoast.com

– – –

Take Your Soul on a Vacation

Visit **www.HealYourLife.com**® to regroup, recharge, and reconnect with your own magnificence. Featuring blogs, mind-body-spirit news, and life-changing wisdom from Louise Hay and friends.

Visit **www.HealYourLife.com** today